Famous Fly-Fishing Adventures

April 2020

JERRY ESTRUTH

PAGE PUBLISHING, INC.
Conneaut Lake, PA

First originally published by Page Publishing 2020

ISBN 978-1-6624-0844-1 (pbk)
ISBN 978-1-6624-0845-8 (digital)

Printed in the United States of America

Contents

Introduction

The first recollection I have was fishing with my dad at Mt. Lassen in Northern California and then at Tuolumne Meadows in Yosemite in the California Sierras when I was five years old. One of my favorite pictures is of him and me standing with the famous Lembert Dome in the background. I was holding about a 6-inch fish, and we were both smiling. That was my first trout. I remember that he was fishing downstream from me, and I went upstream from him and threw some rocks into the stream. He said that I shouldn't throw rocks into the river as I would scare the fish. I told him that I was scaring the fish so they'd swim down to where he was. Later on, I have taken each of my children to photograph them in front of the same dome.

Jerry at Mt. Lassen

Tom and Jerry at Tuolumne Meadows

Over the years, we had many good times because he loved to fish, and I loved to be with him and he with me. When I was about seven, I caught a seventeen-pound striped bass in Frank's tract up in the Sacramento Delta. It was such a nice fish that the local paper put a photo of me in the sport's section. Newspapers, in those days, were family friendly and did those kinds of things.

My dad loved to fish for trout with his old bamboo pole and an automatic reel. He would have been a tremendous nymph fisherman, but we didn't have those in those days, so we fished with salmon eggs. Back then, the Department of Fish and Game had set a limit of fifteen trout, and we usually limited out. Nobody had heard of catch and release. We had a lot of fun.

I recently finished a book by a man whose name would be familiar to you. This gentleman talked about fishing mostly in California before and after World War I. His short book is interesting because he talked about the equipment and the difficulties of traveling around when there were not any interstates and only dirt roads. What was striking, however, was the amount of space he dedicated to the number of fish he caught, their size, and how much they weighed. He described one trip he took that was a combined hunting and fishing trip. The amount of game they shot and the number of fish they caught were amazing.

I started catching and releasing fish during the 1960s when I realized that I could clean a stream out if I kept fish. I decided that a live fish was better than a dead one. Today, that is the norm among fly-fishers, and I know the sport, and the fish are better for it.

My dad died before we had the money to take destination trips, and I have always regretted that. He would have loved to see the beautiful places that I have been lucky enough to see, and he would have loved to have caught the number of mostly large fish I have caught in sweet water and in the salt.

I have friends who always turn up their noses at fishing in the ocean and never have realized how strong the saltwater fish are. Furthermore, it is always good to go to warm climates about February when it is colder than heck up north.

This book describes a lot of the many adventures I have had around the world, chasing sneaky and elusive fish in the most beautiful places there are. I'm beginning to run low on time and energy, but I still have places on my bucket list.

In most cases, I fly-fish, but sometimes, as you will see, I do fish with hardware.

My hope is that you will have fun with this book.

Jeff Wilkes and the Frigate Bird

We were three and a half hours south of Hawaii, and the big jet was banking over Christmas Island in preparation for landing. The blast of hot tropical air hit us as the plane's doors were opened after taxiing up to the tin-covered shed, which passed for customs. We got into the back of some pickup trucks and passed through the small community of Banana, and headed for our hotel, which was a converted officers' barracks from World War II when this island was a major South Pacific Air Force Center. Jeff and I were lucky, as we had requested an open-air bungalow on the beach where we could hear the soft and hypnotizing sounds of the surf. The bungalow was well screened, but if we left the door open, the sand crabs that covered the entire island would invade us.

Jerry and Jeff

9

We had an afternoon orientation from Big Eddy, the chief guide, and he told us to "strip, strip, strip" as we sight cast in front of the big bones of Christmas Island. We all piled into the back of another pickup and headed for some lagoons for an afternoon of bonefishing. This particular afternoon, we were blind casting for our first taste of Christmas Island's "bones." Jeff and I were working around the edge of some deep water and were picking up a few fish that blindly hit our Crazy Charlies and Crystal Puffs.

Of course, we didn't have a clue as to what we were doing, but we were having a good time doing it. We were flush with the excitement of being in warm weather, warm water, and the beauty of the tropics. We were sweating from the exertion in the moist, water-laden air. I wasn't paying much attention to Jeff, which is the way I prefer to fish, when out of the blue, I heard him yell. I looked to where he was, and I saw him running across the sand in pursuit of his rod and reel, which were being transported into the far distance by a large frigate bird. Jeff launched himself in a headlong and, ultimately, futile attempt to catch his rod as it was dragged along the sand. As he did his face-plant in the sand, the frigate bird carried his rod across the sand and over the water. It was an amazing sight: Jeff in the sand and the frigate bird trailing about 30 feet of line attached to a brand-new $700 sage rod, reel, and line as it flew across the lagoon and out of sight.

I ran over to Jeff, trying not to laugh at the incredible sight. Between a series of choice words, he managed to say that after releasing a "bone," he started letting out line in preparation for a new cast. On the backcast, he felt a snag on his line that was unusual on a treeless island where there was nothing to interfere with a backcast. Then the backcast began to pull, and, in surprise, he let his grip go loose on the rod. The frightened bird chose this time to take off from its hovering position and fly away. As they say, the rest was history.

Jeff, of course, proceeded to have the greatest story of the trip, which was good, as he always has great stories to supplement his fishing abilities. He posted a reward to see if any islander could get his rod and reel back, and this resulted in zippo. One guide thought he saw a frigate bird rising and falling in an unusual way, and we spent one afternoon chasing this bird in a leaky raft. Fortunately, we all had extra rods and reels, and Jeff could continue fishing, which, all our hype to the contrary, he does quite well. He bought a loop reel from a guy named Stuart from Florida, who claimed to catch the biggest fish of the trip. He was the kind of guy that always caught the big fish when no one was around to check it out, but he had plenty of good reels to sell. Jeff borrowed a rod from a guy named Johnny, who was their compliments of the Scott Rod Company.

All in all, it was another great adventure and another great story that fills our memory banks. We all caught a lot of large bonefish, and it laid the foundation for a subsequent trip to Christmas Island that was good for many more stories.

Jerry and Jeff enjoying a brew and the warm water

Jeff Wilkes and the Biggest Bonefish in the World

Sometimes, we fly fishermen have quirky habits, and not everyone is as perfect as I. It always reminds me of that old saw that "all fishermen are liars, except for you and me, and sometimes, I'm not so sure about you." Our good friend and fine fisherman Jeff Wilkes tended to be that way.

We met Jeff and the frigate bird, and although that trip took place over 40 years ago, we, meaning Dave Oke, Chris Reidel, Keith Munger, and I, have heard the story of the biggest bonefish in the world almost every time we have gotten together with Jeff, every time we all go fishing.

Jeff was fishing with Tomorrow, one of the guides on Christmas Island. You really do need a guide, for they have great eyes that can see the "ghosts of the flats." If you've never fished Christmas, you should do yourself a favor and give it a try. I have heard, over the years, that the fishing has deteriorated some because of the merciless pressure. I find it hard to believe that the endless miles of flats could ever run out of fish, but anyplace can be overfished.

Unlike the Caribbean, the bones at Christmas tend to be big, solitary fish that travel alone. Stalking them is fun and almost becomes an art form. There are times when you can find a break in the coral and watch fish travel at intervals through the hole right into your casting window. All you have to do is cast and wait until a fish comes along. Then it is strip, strip, strip, and he is on it, takes it, and the fish spools you two or three times. They can run 100 yards quicker and slicker than snot, and you have to have a lot of practice handling your line. You also have to learn to keep your fingers away from the knob on your reel, or you will bust your knuckles.

We also speculate that the bones tend to be bigger on Christmas because Christmas is downwind from Eniwetok, the island that was home to so many H-bomb explosions during the fifties, and we figure that the bones got mutated. Whatever, they are big.

Anyway, Jeff was off fishing by himself along with Tomorrow, and after returning to our prearranged meeting place, he laid claim to having caught the biggest bonefish in the world. Maybe so, but no one saw it except Tomorrow, and his credibility and English were always in question.

Throughout all the years since then, the story never fails to come up whenever we are discussing the merits of big fish and telling stories over bourbon or other adult beverages. In fact, we have started to finish his story for him as he claims that of the four fish in the procession to come through this particular break in the coral, the fish he caught, that "must have gone 10–11 pounds," was the smallest of the four.

Everyone has the right to tell stories, and Jeff can spin some of the best, so we give him a lot of sh———t. All the same, Jeff is a great guy to fish with, drink with, and since he is not the only one among us who has a tendency toward stretching the truth, we have decided to continue to put up with him for as long as we all are able to stand up, hold a rod, and cast a fly to a rising, or cruising, fish.

Chris Reidel, David Oke, Jerry, and Three Very Large Trevally

While Jeff was off catching the biggest bonefish of all time, Chris, David, and I decided to take another kind of adventure. The first time we had gone to Christmas, we learned that it was possible to go outside the reef to the blue water and go after some big fish with some big tackle. Although we loved fly-fishing, we also, as the gentle reader has seen, were not beneath going after bigger prey when we could. So I had packed into our gear, three surf rods that I have had for a while, along with some large spinning reels. I bought some special lures that looked like big bait. I couldn't believe that they cost $10–$12 apiece, but nothing stands in the way of a dedicated, fantasizing, and panting fisherman. It was a funny sight, carrying a 12-foot long tube through all the airports. My surf rods were of the older type and didn't have the split in the middle like the newer ones but had almost 10 feet of the rod before the break.

So we talked to Big Eddy, the chief guide, and he agreed that we could go outside the reef to see what we could catch. We rode the punt, as the motored craft there are called, from the town of London, which is at the tip of the island, right at the mouth of the harbor where the lagoon breaks into the Pacific. We dumped Jeff on one of the huge flats so he could catch the biggest bonefish in the world and proceeded out into the ocean. As soon as we got outside of the harbor, the large Pacific swells began to rock the boat. To understand this situation, you have to get a picture of the punt. It's about 20 feet long, 8 feet wide, and has a sun shelter about 8 feet above the deck. You can either get under it to get out of the sun or, as in our case, stand on it to get a better cast at the large fish that we knew to be there.

So, picture this, David, who was 6'4" and 225 pounds, Chris, who was 6'0" tall and 180 pounds, and I, who was 6'4" and 210 pounds, were on the three parts of this craft—front, back, and on top—ready to go. We all had 11-inch poles with big lures at the end of the line. Chris was on top of the punt, dangling his lure over the ocean when a barracuda about 8 feet long suddenly jumped clear out of the water in front of us and snapped at his lure.

"Did you see that?" we all shouted at the same time, as the great, vicious, and hungry fish splashed back into the water.

The guides shouted that the birds were working just down the coast from where we were. We headed there, full of great anticipation. When we got there, we all started casting and retrieving as fast as we could. We crashed our rods together, thankfully without breaking them, and it must have been hilariously funny to see these three big guys trying to stand up in the rocking boat, waving these rods frantically, and retrieving as fast as they could, trying to catch a fish.

Then it happened—we had a threefer. Here we were, playing three huge and strong fish at the same time, trying not to fall off the boat. There were big fish in that water, and they were hungry, and we didn't want to be bait. Finally, we landed 150 collective pounds of trevally, a wonderfully beautiful and strong fish.

Chris, David, and Jerry

We continued to fish for a while and caught a couple more beautiful fish, but the threefer was to be remembered and not repeated.

The best part was yet to come. We did bonefishing for the afternoon, heard about the biggest bonefish in the world, and finally returned to the hotel for cocktails, more lies, and great stories about the biggest bone in the world. The chef prepared for our dinner a huge plate, meaning about twenty-four inches long, 12 inches wide, and fifteen inches high, full of the freshest, most delicious trevally sashimi you could ever hope to have. It was a fantastic end to a fantastic day. We all had stories to tell even though they all ended with the biggest bone in the world.

David Oke kissing a giant trevally

Chris Reidel, David Oke, Jerry, and the Trout Pond

One day on a fisherman's club weekend, Chris Reidel, David Oke, and I were trying to win the big fish contest. The rules for this tournament were pretty simple: he who catches the big fish wins the prize.

On the theory that we could catch a big trout in big water, we went up to Lake Almanor early in the morning and rented a motorboat and proceeded to fish all day. It was one of those beautiful sierra days when the sun is golden, the air is pure, the water is calm, and the fishermen are ready. Unfortunately, and it's why they call it fishing, not catching, the fish were in no mood to cooperate. We flogged the water mercilessly with our trolling rigs, realizing as the morning went on that we had no idea what we were doing. All of us were basically fly fishermen, and knowing that flies in this environment would do nothing to a big fish, we tried hardware, another misadventure.

We trolled around, we drank beer, we crossed the lake, we fished shallow, we fished deep, we drank more beer, we ate sandwiches, and we did everything else we could think of to scare up at least a little fish. About noon, we decided that we needed a potty break and beached this boat on a piece of shoreline across the lake from the lodge that we had started from. There we discovered a magnificent hatch of swallowtails covering the ground. So we did the logical thing. We had a beer and watched the butterflies for a while. We didn't notice that the wind had come up out on the lake.

If you don't know about Lake Almanor, you must realize that it is a huge lake, and when the wind blows from a certain direction, it can become quite rough, with big waves. Since I had rented the boat, I was the motorman and started back across the huge lake. The water was so rough that we didn't fish at all and were just trying to get back across the water. Chris huddled up under the covered prow while David bravely kept his face to the wind. We were glad the boat was covered as we still took on water. At every bounce, I thought the boat would break apart. I tried to quarter as best I could, but I was afraid the boat would broach and turn over. As the afternoon wore on, I wondered if we were making any headway whatsoever. I guess we did, because, although beat to hell, we finally got back to our marina and got off the boat.

We had another beer and bemoaned the fact that we had nothing to show for a hard day's effort and that the one hundred members of the fisherman's club would laugh their collective butts off if we went back with no fish. We were an hour from home and started to think about where we might be able to fish on the way. Someone, I'm not sure who, remembered that we saw a sign for a trout pond somewhere on the way. Not liking this very much, we all decided that we should go there and see what was what.

We had another beer and hit the road. About halfway back, we saw the sign for the trout pond and hung a quick left off the road and proceeded up a short dirt track to the pond. We got to the place and found a Vietnam vet in a wheelchair, sitting out in front of his doublewide. We pulled up, got out, and greeted our host. Well, I guess I'd be surly too, if I was in a wheelchair, sitting out in front of a double-wide next to a trout pond. He kind of grunted that if we caught one, it was ours, and it was $5 a pound for the fish. So Chris and David started to cast flies out in the middle of these fish in the pond. I was so embarrassed. I stood as far away as I could and watched the action. They had a lot of fish on and played them until they got off. One monster fish took Chris's fly, and he played him for a while. This was the biggest fish in the pond, and the vet wheeled over to watch. This fish finally broke off and started to swim away. It swam about 15 feet and turned belly up. We tried to revive it, we prayed over it, we pleaded with the fish gods, but the vet said it was ours.

We weighed it, and it weighed in at 11 pounds. It was so old that its poor fins were shredded, and the body was in terrible shape. Well, after paying for this monster, we had to decide what to do with it. We bought the vet a beer and had one all around while we contemplated this disaster. We decided that we had to enter the fish in the contest, as there were no rules about where you had to catch the fish. We were all so embarrassed that we drew straws to see who would enter the fish. David drew the short straw, and so he was the one to enter the fish.

We drove back to the lodge, had another beer with a Jack Daniel's chaser while we got up enough nerve to get the fish out of the car. Then inspiration struck. Somebody said that since David had won the big fish contest the year before, that he could enter the fish and decline the prize by disqualifying himself from the contest as he thought it bad form to win two years in a row. We all thought that this was a marvelous plan, so we got this ratty old fish out of the car and marched proudly up to the scales. Everyone wanted to know where we caught it, so we told them that we had found this little tributary to the Feather River and just dappled a fly in a little tiny hole, and this huge monster fish grabbed the fly, and the rest was history. Everyone was so wasted (this is a group of serious drinkers) that this story seemed eminently plausible, and everyone thought David was wonderful for disqualifying himself from the contest.

We all were laughing so hard. We could hardly contain ourselves, so we had more Jack Daniel's. By this time, we were calling him John, as he was becoming our good friend.

At the prize ceremony after dinner, everyone waited with bated breath while the prizes were announced. I forget who took first place, but Chris and I won second and third place because we had caught big fish on the second day of the tournament. We got nice prizes, and David was feeling left out. Then out of the blue came the announcement from the superior court judge who was president that year. He announced proudly that he had created a special prize for a fisherman who exemplified the outstanding qualities of a true fisherman quality such as honor, truthfulness, charity, and generosity. He went on, at length, how this fisherman had every right to claim the first prize as he had caught the biggest fish but was too magnanimous and thoughtful to deprive others of the big prize because he had won it the year before. He then called David up and continued on at length about what a wonderful, fine, and generous man he was and how he deserved the undying praise and admiration of the entire group.

Chris and I almost choked on our John Daniel's. David was laughing his ass off and saying that he really didn't deserve it, but in the true spirit of a member of the fisherman's club, he would accept it on behalf of everyone he had ever met and assured the judge that the qualities that he espoused could be found in the heart of every true fisherman.

David sat down, bought us some drinks, and we all eventually retired and swore that the secret would remain safe until this day.

Another Big Fish Contest at the Fisherman's Club

The fisherman's club has a long and storied past. It has been going on a fishing trip somewhere each year since about 1927. The group is composed of pretty good fellows, and usually, everyone has a good time. Actually, today, about half the group plays golf, and the other half goes fishing. The rules of the fishing contest have changed over the years, and instead of just three prizes, we now try to give away as many prizes as we can.

There are prizes for the biggest two fish from large lakes, the biggest two fish from small lakes, the biggest two fish from rivers, etc. Then there are prizes for anyone who might have come in third or fourth. There is a prize for the guy who fell out of his boat, straddled the dock/boat before he fell in, drank so much he couldn't fish, etc.

David and Jerry

One year, I managed to piss everyone off, which added to the lore of the club, by catching a 5-inch fish in the middle fork of the Feather River. Nobody entered a fish in this part of the contest because they were too embarrassed. I, on the other hand, had been embarrassed by experts and had absolutely no qualms about entering such a puny insignificant fish. My fish took first prize in this category. I endured a ton of derision and hoots and hollers, but I claimed my prize anyway. It was an excellent fly-tying kit that nobody else wanted.

Since I wrote the rules, I always had said that *every* fish should be entered into the contest so everyone had a chance to win. Drunken souls that they are, they never bothered to read the rules. So since I wrote them, I had a huge advantage over them.

Since we have been giving more and more prizes away, we have gotten more fishermen interested in fishing, which is the whole object of the trip. We have also started to give prizes for the guy who catches and releases most fish (environmental), the guy with the best fish story, and the guy who lies best about it all.

Mostly though, the grand prize goes to the guy who catches the biggest mackinaw, the biggest brown trout or the biggest rainbow. Since you generally need a boat to get the big ones, sometimes fishermen are dissed and berated for using a guide who has a boat. Egomaniacs that we are, most of us don't give a flying f——k in a rolling doughnut what the others think.

All in all, it's a man's tournament for men, and a good time is had by all.

David Oke's First Fly-Fishing Lesson

Back about 1984, David Oke and I had been discussing fishing, and he wanted to learn how to fly-fish. I told him that the best place to learn would be on the Madison River in Montana—a beautiful river, hungry trout, big sky, wonderful stars, camping by the river at the Wade Lakes Bridge, and talking to an old and ancient cowboy named Frank Shaw. Frank charged $3 a night to camp by the river in our van, and for a price of a beer or two would tell stories far into the night. It is still called "Three Dollar Bridge."

He talked about the great Yellowstone earthquake of the late 1950s when a lot of people died, and the Madison ran dry because of the formation of a new lake called Quake Lake. A whole mountainside came down, buried many campers, and formed a brand-new lake. Although today, the fishing in the "slide" is magnificent, in those worrisome days, nobody knew if the "slide" was going to give way and flood everyone downstream or not. As it was, the Army Corps dug a spillway and restored the river the best they could while leaving the lake intact. The fishing was better all the way around. It was very good in 1984, long before the advent of the whirling disease, which had taken such a toll on the rainbows of the Madison.

So I figured that David, who had had a couple of fly-fishing lessons, was ready for the big time. We hiked down about 3 miles on the south side of the Madison from the bridge, and I told David to start fishing up while I fished behind him about 50 yards. After an hour or so, I started to hear many words that sounded like swear words. I started to watch David, and he was missing fish after fish. He was too slow on the set, but at least he was getting bites. I, on the other hand, was catching fish after fish, making David, who was just barely competitive, madder and madder. It was one of those days when my royal wolf was magic. I had an incredibly hot hand and was hammering the bank feeders.

Finally, while I was landing a fish, I heard "Oh f——" and I looked up just in time to see David throw his rod and reel about as far back onto the shore as he could. He sat down and said that his rod didn't work, and he didn't want to fish anymore. I walked up to him and said that my rod seemed to be working perfectly and that he should try mine. After a few minutes of hemming and hawing, he agreed. I went back onto the bank, inspected the rod that didn't work, and started fishing back behind David as he continued. I think my rod was just a little bit quicker, and he started to catch the trout for which the Madison is famous. I took a lot of fish on his rod, and by the time it got dark, we had had a great day fishing, and it was time for dinner—Jack Daniel's and coffee.

The old three dollar bridge.

After our nourishing dinner, we got into my old VW pop-top and started telling lies. After more of Jack Daniel's, David had to go outside to answer the call of nature. After about thirty seconds, he came lunging back into the van and said that we were being invaded by Nazguls as in *The Lord of the Rings*. We all piled out and saw that one half of the sky was covered by the Milky Way and a bazillion stars. The other half looked like a big dark bird with its beak pointed directly at the van. It looked like it was attacking.

Of course, they were clouds, but it really was mysterious. We call that "The Night of the Nazguls." David had been gone ten years now, and I missed him.

Tunja, Colombia (1965)

Back about 1965, when I was in the Peace Corps in Colombia, South America, I met a Lebanese ex-patriot, whose name I forgot after fifty-five years, and we struck up a fine conversation about fishing in Colombia. Coincidentally, he loved to fish, so we found that we had a lot in common.

Back in those days, I wasn't particularly only interested in fly-fishing, so we decided to go after some trout in a special place that he knew about. The lake was called Pontezuela, which was about a four- to five-hour drive from Bogota, the capital city. He had lived in Colombia for some time and knew the country quite well.

Actually, the fishing was quite good, and we had a good time. We trolled around, and the bite was on.

I was young then and was wearing my ruana.

The Colombians were trying to restore the fishery, so they had a feeder stream stocked with brood trout where we couldn't fish, but it was legal to fish in the lake itself.

So we made the trip. We were dressed for a cold country. Most people think that since Colombia is in the tropics and near the equator, that is always hot; however, there are many temperate and cold zones. They are called thermoclines, and there is a place in Santa Marta where you can stand in the warm water of the Caribbean and see snowcapped peaks.

My group of Peace Corps volunteers was tasked with forming cooperatives for economic development, and I have always regretted that I didn't know enough about saltwater fishing, for I think I would have liked to investigate and start a fishing cooperative on the coast of the Caribbean. The fishing on the Colombian coast couldn't have been much different from Los Roques in Venezuela. There had to have been bonefish, peacock bass, and who knows what else. It would have been groundbreaking, so to speak, and would have opened up a whole new enterprise for the poor Colombian fishermen on the coast.

"Those were the days, my friends, we thought they'd never end."

Guatavita

In the same neck of the woods as Tunja and our fishing adventure is the famous Colombian Lake of Guatavita.

Guatvita Lake

Legend has it that about one thousand years ago, there was a group of indigenous people called the Muisca that used this lake as a sacred spot.

Their leader or "zipa" used to cover his body in gold dust and then would wash it all off in the lake, thereby covering the bottom of the lake with gold. Furthermore, he would throw golden figurines into the water.

The Spanish, when they arrived, heard legends of a lake of gold and, of course, went there to find it. They tried in vain to drain the lake, as you can see from the V-shaped opening in the rim, but nobody had been able to do that. We didn't fish there but marveled at the story and the beauty of it.

Bringing Clean Ice from Tulum

Several years ago, David and I went fishing at Punta Allen, several hours by car south of Cancun. We were part of a group of eleven fisherpeople that comprised a group led by a local fly-fishing trip arranging business. An American woman ran the lodge that we stayed at, and by reputation, we were going to get the best of food and accommodations. We rented cars in Cancun and started our trip south. We convoyed about halfway down the coast and stayed at the Blue Parrot Lodge, where we were treated to a wonderful beach full of topless bathers. A wonderful place it was.

At dinner, the group gathered for some wonderful Mexican food, and the frozen margaritas flowed freely. I sipped my beer and drank no water. Everyone laughed at me, but old Peace Corps habits die hard. Back in the day, I spent five years in South America without getting any kind of serious dysentery. In our training, we were taught to avoid anything that was not boiled, canned, baked, cooked, bottled, or sterilized. Most of all, we were taught that all surface water and ice, unless treated, were to be avoided.

The next day, we followed our leader down through the surf near the Blue Parrot while he tried to bring up something from the waves. It, although a beautiful morning, was a fruitless effort. We finally saddled up and drove on down the coast to our fishing destination. Here it was more of the same. There were lots of margaritas with cold ice in our drinks. Once again, I was laughed at because I was a pussy. I was told more than once that the ice was safe because the American owner actually went to the trouble of bringing the ice in from Tulum, a city a couple of hours away. What a joke! The water there was just as bad as it was where we were. In fact, the local doctor had to evacuate a child while we were there and take him into Cancun because he was suffering from typhoid fever.

While swimming in the surf in front of our lodge, there was a noticeable smell of sewage about the water. But everyone continued to drink the water, and I was the oddball because I treated my water and was careful about what I ate and drank.

Everything went fine until about day 4 when I was the only one who could go out fishing. I wish I had caught a million fish, but I just had an average day. The next day, only one other fisherman was able to go out. The others were all going from each end. Needless to say, their trip was pretty well shot. I don't know why it's so hard for people to discipline themselves for a few days in order to stay healthy.

They never did admit that it might have been the water or the ice from Tulum, and they all wound up blaming it on some of the pasta salad that they ate on day 2.

Jerry's Bonefishing Trip to Cozumel

Back in the days when I was single, not by choice, but by ex-wife, I enjoyed a pleasant interlude with a friend down Mexico way in Cozumel before Hurricane Gilbert had ravaged it. We had a great time. She knew a small and intimate residencia that we stayed at, which was just a five-minute walk from the plaza.

We went snorkeling and sunning. We rented a jeep and toured the entire area, getting eaten alive by mosquitoes when we visited a remote Mayan temple in the middle of the island. As the road turned on the windward side of the island, we stopped at a little *sitio*, where we could have coldish beer and Mescal. I don't think we drank the worm, but we had a great time.

One afternoon as we were walking along the main drag, I looked into a sportfishing store and saw a fly rod. Curious, I went in and asked what you caught with that. Bonefish (*espinazo*), I was told. In those days, I really hadn't experienced bonefish but had heard that they were hot fish. I inquired about a guide, and we got set to go the next morning.

The next morning, bright and early, I showed up with the only fishing clothes I had—Levi's and tennis shoes. The guide asked if he should bring cerveza and how much. I said *bastante* (enough), so he brought fifteen *Coronita, la Bonita* (pretty Coronas). As it turned out, that was barely enough. On the dock, I had the first beer. "Desayuno de Campeones," I told him. Breakfast of champions.

We then proceeded to plow through rather heavy seas for about two hours to the very northern tip of the island. We then went through a windy winding waterway to get back into what were very sandy flats. We started to chase the bones.

It was so hot and humid. I was wet from the Levi's, and the fishing rod was such a wimpy stick that I decided that it was going to be a tough day of fishing. Adding to that was the fact that the fishing line was made of some indeterminate material, and the flies were not particularly made for bonefishing. The guide knew nothing about bones and bonefishing, and I was on my own.

It took about two hours of stalking groups of bonefish before I saw a couple that were tailing. I pitched my fly to them, and one struck. The reel was so old that the drag hardly functioned at all, and I broke him off really quick. Of course, we had to have a couple of beers to celebrate. To make a long story longer, I was full of sand and silt and not too happy with the equipment, so I had another beer.

At the end of the day, I had taken and released about six to eight bones and had gotten a real taste of what bonefishing could be like. We then plowed back through some heavy ocean to get back to town. Of course, more beer was consumed so that the ride wouldn't seem so choppy.

When we arrived at the dock, the guide counted the bottles consumed. He had had one, and I had downed fourteen.

It was a wonder that I could still fish. Or as they, "If you've ever been too drunk to fish, you must be from Bakersfield." I guess I've never been to Bakersfield.

Foul Mouth Guides Cursing in Front of Children

It's hard to ruin a day of fishing with your son, but occasionally it happens. It started out to be a great day, and I suppose that in the final analysis, it ended that way, but we had to work at it.

We stopped at Denny's to have breakfast, and Nicholas and I downed our share of pancakes and bacon and anticipated a great day of fishing ahead of us. On our way out, we passed a bank of pay phones, and I told Nick that he had better check the coin returns to see if there was any money in them. He said he thought that was a silly thing to do, but I told him to do it anyway. In the coin return of the third phone, he found $7.65 worth of coins that someone had left behind. He and I couldn't believe it. Usually, you picked up a couple of dimes or quarters, but in all my years of checking, I had never found much more than $0.75 or so. We *knew* right then that it was going to be a great day of fishing.

We motored on to the Redding Fly Shop, where I had spent many wonderful days with their guides on the Lower Sacramento, catching beautiful, healthy trout. We had a new guide for the day, one that I had never fished with before. The day started out as they usually do with a bit of chatter and stuff down by the river. I told him that I had invented a new way of fishing wet flies by putting a small split shot on the bottom of the string of flies (nymphs). The split shot, if it gets snagged, as it does a lot on the Lower Sac, would pull off, and you wouldn't lose all your gear. He said that that was cool but illegal. I didn't feel like arguing with him for the fish and game rules in California, specifically state that small weights were fine at the end of your line. I wasn't going to start off on a wrong foot with this guy.

We rigged up and started fishing. It wasn't long before we discovered that this guide had one of the foulest mouths that I have heard in a long time. I'm not, by any means, a prude and have been known to hurl invective at fish, poles, trees, line, snarls, hooks, boats, anchors, tackle boxes, etc. In fact, there was a great fishing commercial one time that featured a guy throwing all his tackle, including his motor out of his boat. I could really identify with that guy.

At all times, however, I have tried to avoid swearing in front of children and women. I have always thought that kids, especially males, will learn soon enough what kinds of words are effective in certain situations.

This guide, however, sometime around noon, decided that swearing would help catch fish or something like that. Then it was a decision about letting him do his own thing and try to make sure that he got us over fish or simply ask him to cease and desist. To make matters worse, the guy was a smoker, and between cigarettes and smokeless tobacco, he really began to make an ass of himself. I caught my trout and missed a couple of large ones, but my son was having a hard day. It came down to me to try to help him catch a couple of fish. In the middle of the afternoon, Nick caught, and I couldn't believe this, a sucker. He was so proud of this fish, and I feared that the guide would take the wind out of his sails. At least he had enough class to avoid doing that. And then, on the very next cast, Nick caught another sucker. In all my years fishing the Lower Sacramento, I had never even seen a sucker. Oh yeah, we all knew they were in there, but to hook them on floating tiny nymphs seemed to me to be impossible.

Nick was extremely happy and was looking forward to getting a trout, and he kept on fishing hard throughout the rest of the day but landed no more fish; however, he had a big trout on for about twenty minutes before it broke off and was thrilled. The trout was hooked, and so was Nick.

The guide, who shall remain nameless, continued to pepper his speech with ample four-letter words. He got no tip and would get no further business from me. I would rather not fish than go with this jerk, and that is saying something. He's still fishing out of there but has developed a reputation of being a total asshole. What goes around comes around.

Nick and I still had great day fishing.

David Oke and the Big Permit

Fly-fishing is a strange and wonderful undertaking. It can sometimes be awfully humbling. Punta Allen was such a time. You may remember the trip to Punta Allen, where they brought in the ice from Tulum, and an American ran the lodge. Well, the fishing was not great but totally adequate.

The first morning, David and I arrived at the pier with our poles in one hand and a Corona in the other. "Desayuno de Campeones," I said. Breakfast of Champions. The Mexican guides laughed with us, and we hopped into Augustin's panga and headed off to the mangroves where we hoped to catch bones, permit, snook, and/or tarpon.

The morning was absolutely beautiful. The sea was calm, the birds were wheeling in the early morning light, the air was warm, and we were hot to catch fish. As we got close to the mangroves, we passed a flat where there must have been one thousand pink flamingos feeding. What an absolutely gorgeous and memorable morning! I didn't know how memorable it was going to be.

Augustin started poling through the mangroves, admonishing us to be absolutely quiet. We were going to stalk permit, the legendary fish that only a couple of hundred people had ever taken on a fly. David and I flipped a coin to see who was going to have the first shot at the first fish. David won and picked up a rod with a long colorful fly on it. Augustin had rigged four poles, two with colorful flies and two with crabs. David and I, being fat, dumb and happy, didn't know yet that crabs were to be used for the permit.

So as it turned out, David was holding a pole with a tarpon fly on it. I sat down, David stood up, and we waited while Augustin poled silently through the mangroves. Suddenly, Augustin said, "There's a permit."

We looked, and there, about 20 feet away, was the gorgeous permit, and the only permit David and I had ever seen. I muttered something like, "Gees, David, you could fall into a pile of sh—t and come out smelling like a rose."

Anyway, David cautiously let out some line and threw a perfect cast about 3 feet off the permit's nose. The fly slowly sank, looking delicious. The permit looked at it and, I swear, threw it a sneering look, and slowly swam away.

"Hijo de madre," said Augustin.

Maybe I'll get a shot, I thought. David said something that is not printable.

Then it was my turn. David gave me the pole, and I stood up and was ready. David sat down, muttering about the injustice of it all.

Augustin kept poling, silently through the mangroves. I was ready. David was pissed.

A few minutes later, the permit came back. It moved slowly and silently to its familiar position about 20 feet from the boat. I stripped line and laid the fly out to a perfect position, about 15 inches from the permit's nose. The fly sank slowly. The permit looked at it and swam disdainfully out of sight. Then the unthinkable happened. Augustin shouted something like, "You stupid gringo, how could you be using a tarpon fly to catch a permit."

"But," I stammered, "David was using the same fly, and how come you didn't notice it then?"

"I didn't notice it" was his only reply.

Then it was David's turn. He chuckled as he took the correct pole with the crab attached. "Luck of the draw" was his consoling comment.

You can guess the rest of the story. The permit came back. David made a perfect cast to it with the crab. The permit lunched it, and after forty-five minutes of a wonderful fight through the mangrove, David had landed a beautiful 25 pound permit. I wasn't too pissed off. I smiled as I took his picture and congratulated him on playing him well. It was hard to do because, throughout the fight, David kept telling me how wonderful it was to have such a beautiful fish at the end of his line.

The fishing gods must have been mad at me that day. Why didn't Augustin see the stupid tarpon fly when David threw it at the permit? Why didn't we know beforehand that permit only ate crabs and not tarpon flies?

Somehow, and unknowingly, I must have pissed off the fishing gods.

Unfortunate, but it's another wonderful fishing story. At least, I didn't have to spend two days sitting on the toilet while my buddy was out catching fish.

A Young Boy and His First Fly

Once upon a time, there was a little boy trying to catch trout out of a beautiful stream called the Stanislaus high in the Sierras of California. This seven-year-old was walking along the bank with his steel-telescoping pole equipped with a level-wind reel and some old salmon eggs that he was using for bait.

He was not having a good day and was getting tired. He hadn't hooked even one fish, and his hands were stinky and sticky from continually putting salmon eggs on his #12 hook and immediately losing them in the fast water of the river. As he moved along, he did notice that there were fish jumping here and there, but none of the trout would even glance at his bait.

Discouraging was not quite the proper word to describe the situation, but the little guy felt awfully alone and mighty sad.

Fishing near the Old Strawberry Hotel and barns, circa 1930.   *Courtesy Ola Zimmerman Collection*

As he wandered along the stream, he noticed that up ahead, there was a man waving his pole over his head. From time to time, the waving stopped, and the man pulled up a fish.

"What was this guy doing?" he asked himself. Finally, he got closer and closer and ultimately got up enough nerve to get right beside the man. He dropped his egg into the water, and nothing happened again.

The man looked down and asked him, "How ya doing?"

"Not very well," the little boy replied.

"How'd ya like to catch a real fish?" the man asked.

Well, the boy thought, *that is a real dumb question*, but answered, "It'd be mighty nice to catch a fish."

The man said that in order to catch a fish, you had to use flies like the one he had at the end of his line. The man pulled up his line and showed the boy a fly that he called a gray hackle peacock. "This is what you have to use," he explained.

It turned out that this man was Danny DiVitorio, who had a cabin up the road from the boy's.

He reached into his pocket and pulled out a square box. When he opened it, the boy saw that it was full of pretty colored flies. The man poked around in the box and finally pulled out a gray hackle peacock.

"Let me tie it on your line," he said.

I watched him as he tied it on and said that I would have to learn to tie knots just like that one. Then he stood up, pointed out at the water, and said to just throw the fly out on the water. "But first," he said, "you have to promise me that you will throw the German Browns back. They are native to this stream, and a good fisherman can nearly wipe them out." The little boy promised, and the man smiled. "There," he said as a trout jumped. "Put the fly there."

The little boy tried mightily to get the fly out there, and miraculously, it flew out near where the man had pointed. At that point, the boy knew that there must be a God somewhere because a mighty fish jumped out of the water and inhaled the fly. The boy either set the hook with great reflexes, or the fish hooked himself, but after what seemed like a mighty battle, the fish came to the man's net.

That night, and it was a warm summer night, the boy and the man fished until dark, and it was time to go home. The man had a cabin near the boy's cabin, and they walked home together.

"Think you'd like to learn to fly-fish?" asked the man.

"You bet," replied the boy.

That night, the fish weren't the only thing hooked as the boy was hooked on fly-fishing from that day forth.

Thirty years later, that boy, now a man, was walking along the same stretch of water. He had his pole made from the latest generation of graphite, his double taper floating fly line, his Gunnison reel, and his polaroid glasses. His well-worn vest had pockets bulging with fly boxes. He had hip boots on, as the river wasn't big enough for chest waders.

That evening was warm, and he had a hot hand. He had caught and released about 30 fish so far, and he was beginning to draw a crowd that was following him down the bank. There was a good mayfly hatch on, and he was catching a lot of little rainbows and browns. Once he looked down, he saw a little boy who was looking mighty dejected. The boy had an old pole and an older line. He was dunking salmon eggs and was not catching any fish.

"How do you do that?" he asked the man. It was déjà vu all over again as the man flashed back to a similar evening so long ago.

"Well, I'll tell you," the man said. "You see," he said, "this is a fly, and the fish like to eat them. In fact, most of what a trout eats is flies. You see those bugs flying over the water? That's what fish mostly eat. If you want to catch fish, you'll use them. How'd you like to catch a fish?"

"You bet," said the boy.

The man took out a fly box and knelt down next to the boy. Digging through the box, he finally found what he wanted—a gray hackle peacock. He pulled it out and showed it to the boy. He tied some tippet onto the boy's line and then tied the fly on.

"You're going to have to learn to tie these knots if you're going to fly-fish," he said to the boy.

The boy said that was okay with him.

"You can fish with me for a while," the man said, "if you agree to release any German Brown trout that you catch. They're native to this stream, and a good fisherman can take all of them out. They only eat flies, and we have to protect them."

"Okay," said the boy, "let's do it."

The boy and the man fished together for an hour or so, and the boy took a lot of fish. He was a good student and put the fly almost exactly where the man told him. Finally, it was time to quit.

"How old are you?" asked the man.

"Seven," said the boy.

"I knew that," said the man.

This story is true. How do I know? Because I was the first little boy, and I was lucky enough to do a little part to keep the eternal circle unbroken.

Under the Southern Cross

Our expectations were high as we flew across the Straits of Magellan on our way to challenge the big sea-run German Bowns in Tierra del Fuego, Argentina. As we got off the plane in Rio Grande, we were greeted by a blast of wind that was to become our constant companion.

"The wind is your friend," said Miguel and Alejandro, our guides for the week. They helped us get our gear together, took us to the Posada, settled us in, and said that they'd be back about 5:00 p.m. to take us to the river for an evening's fishing. They were prompt, and we were ready. We passed through the river control point, got our licenses, stomped in a box full of lime to kill any bugs we might have on our boots, and went fishing. The first night, my fishing partner Tom and I caught a lot of fish, the biggest being about 10 pounds. What a thrill! Here we were, not knowing what the heck we were doing, fishing for big browns in Argentina, at the other end of the earth! That night, there was almost no wind. We didn't know how lucky we were.

The next day was warm with little wind. Fishing was excellent, we thought, as we each caught several fish up to 14 pounds. We broke for lunch about 1:00 p.m. and retired to a small trailer at streamside where we had hot lunches and two bottles of fine wine for the four of us who wound up fishing together. We noticed that the trailer was tied down with guy wires, and we wondered if we'd ever get to know the legendary winds of Tierra del Fuego. Fishing that evening was good. The weather was warm.

The next morning, the wind, our friend, started to blow. And blow it did. For the next several days, it blew. How windy was it? It was so windy that you could hold your 8 wt graphite IV straight up, and the tip pointed to 10:30 a.m. It was so windy that you had white caps in your wineglass during lunchtime. It was so windy that we understood why the trailer was guyed down. It was so windy that the entire brown tippet of my Teeny 300 line, about 25 feet, blew out horizontally and didn't hit the ground. It was so windy that most of the time, I cast with my rod in a horizontal position, sometimes with my back to the river.

But the fishing was worth it. It seemed that the fishing turned on about 11:00 and turned off about 1:00. In the evening, although we started fishing again about 6:00, the fish didn't begin cooperating until about 8:00 p.m., with the bite continuing until dark, about 9:45 p.m. Being that far south, the sun didn't set until really late in the evening. It was peculiar. The fish would start jumping when the bite turned on. What a sight to see when these fifteen- to twenty-pound fish decided to start jumping clear out of the water just a few feet from where you were fishing.

At dark, we retired from the river, had a warm or cold drink, and marveled at the glories of the Southern Skies: the Southern Cross, the Greater and Lesser Magellanic Clouds, a funny looking Orion with his head pointing down instead of up, and the beauty of the southern Milky Way. After a ride to the Posada, we would have a late dinner and rest for the early morning fishing. What a blast!

In order to fish this river well, a fisherman should be able to cast 60 to 75 feet in extremely windy conditions. Rarely was the wind directly in our faces as we could quarter around to make it easier. I found that a Teeny line was the most effective thing to use. One of my friends used a T200, but I found a T300 that seemed to get me down deeper. A six- to seven-foot tippet worked well as the fish seemed to be near the bottom, which, by the way, was very forgiving without any snags. I varied my stripping methods, but I found the most profitable way was to strip fairly rapidly. Although I took a couple of fish on a dead drift, most of the time, they took on a rapid retrieve. We fished along long banks, and although fish could be taken throughout the beat, it seemed that, with the bite continuing until dark, the most honey holes were near the end of the far bank.

The wildlife was superb. We saw several guanaco, a llama-like animal, several condors, some ibis, some geese, some beavers, and hawks. Since there wasn't a tree to be found for miles around the river, we wondered how the beavers survived but were told that they build their dams in the riverbanks somehow.

The flies that seemed to produce the best were fairly routine: black rubberlegs, bitch creek nymphs, something called a Steve's Sparkle Pupa, and even an egg-sucking leech, all size 4–8. All seemed to work when fished properly. Although I occasionally used these with a floating line, the sinker seemed to fish much better. If you're not sure what flies to take with you, don't worry! There are at least two great fly shops in the town of Rio Grande, a short walk from the hotel. By the way, Tierra del Fuego is a free trade zone, so prices are comparable to the US.

It was a long way to go, but what a great trip! The score for the week made it all worthwhile. While I saw a 24 pounder taken, the biggest I took was only 16 pounds. While that was my biggest, I caught and released about 50 sea-run German Browns over 5 pounds, thirty of them over 10 pounds. They are strong, beautiful, healthy, and well-worth catching fish. Another trip of a lifetime!

Alaska and Dr. Juice

Outside our Room

There was one trip we made to Brooks Lodge in Alaska. You know, that was the spot where the bears all line up on the waterfall and caught the big salmon as they tried to jump up the falls. There was a viewing place that had been built on the side of the river, and it was amazing to stand there and watch these big bears in action. You could see big trout in the water waiting to catch pieces of flesh or eggs stripped from the bigger and dying salmon.

Jeff Wilkes and I went with some fellow stock brokerage buddies, one of whom was Bob Hack, an excellent fly fisherman and bourbon drinker. The first afternoon, he broke out two-fifths of Makers Mark and set them on the table. Then he had to go answer the call of nature. When he came back, one of the bottles was empty, and the second had some serious evaporation problems. "What happened!" he exclaimed, and we all swore that someone we had never seen before had broken in and consumed it. Bob later died in his waders while fishing Silver Creek, Idaho. We miss him.

We were fishing with all kinds of big flies for the big rainbows that would lie just downstream from the spawning salmon. As eggs would escape from the redds, the trout would scarf them up big time. Well, I had a little bottle of Berkeley Strike, some kind of fish attractant that I decided to try. I reasoned that if the trout were taking little egg imitations that didn't stink, they might really come after something that stunk like something fishy. I started using it, and my hookup rate improved dramatically. I thought this was the best thing since sliced bread.

I also was cautious about telling anyone because, at some level, I figured that what I was doing was basically an unethical form of fly-fishing. Although after great emotional and ethical struggles I still wasn't sure, the chance to hammer big trout was simply too great, and I succumbed to temptation and kept catching big fish.

One day, we had a flyout from Brooks Lodge to the Moraine River. As we circled to land, we saw a family of five large bears that were wandering around about where we wanted to fish. Everyone else, Bob Hack, Jeff Wilkes of frigate bird fame, Karl Belavich from Santa Rosa, and I were all on the trip. Everyone else had decided to take a 5 wt rod because the weather was so great at Brooks. I took my 8 wt, just in case of wind or larger water. As a result of this decision, I was able to cast into the driving wind of the Moraine River while the other guys watched their offerings get blown back into their faces. Consequently, I could cover a great deal more water. Fishing was tough, and there were not a lot of redds in the river, so a lot of the trout had already fallen back into the bigger Lake Iliamna that was a couple of miles downstream.

So I decided that, first, I'd fish deep using some little weights and second, use my Berkeley Strike. Well, to make a long story longer, I caught all kinds of fish. My buddies, not being very competitive at all, were getting more agitated every time I would yell, "Fish on!" Of course, I was not doing this to p——them off or anything.

Finally, Bob Hack yelled at me, "Hey, Estruth, what're you using, Dr. Juice?"

He was close but no cigar, and I answered truthfully, "Hey, what kind of fisherman to you think I am?"

It was only several years later that I was able to admit, after several glasses of Jack Daniel's, that I was, in fact, using Berkeley Strike. Unfortunately, Bob Hack never lived long enough to hear the tale. For that, I'm sorry. He was a great fisherman and a good friend.

New Zealand and a Boob Job

Once upon a time, when I was a little boy in what was then the little town of San Jose, California, I used to wander by a travel agency at the corner of First and San Fernando Streets. Of course, it is long gone now, replaced by some very tall buildings, but I still remember the size of the huge trout that was mounted in the window underneath a sign that said, "Visit New Zealand!" I used to go home and look up New Zealand on the globe we had and wonder how I could ever get there, but all I could do was file that little thought in the back of my mind, but I never forgot it.

About the same time, I acquired an interest in astronomy, an interest that, like fly-fishing, has never left me. I remember reading about Halley's Comet in a beginning astronomy book and its incredible appearance during the year of 1910. I noticed that it would be 1986 before it would return. Well, the years went by, and soon 1986 was approaching. As I read the magazines about the reappearance of this great comet, I discovered two things: 1) that it was my luck that this was going to be the worst appearance of the comet in approximately 2,000 years, and 2) that the best place to see it from was New Zealand. So I said to myself, "Self, you have to go fishing in New Zealand and combine the trip with the chance to see Halley's Comet." So I looked around, found a great place called Cedar Safari ran by a wonderful host named Dick Frazier, got on the plane, and went.

Dick Frazier's lodge

Dick Frazier had a beautiful lodge around Wanaka on the South Island with daily fly outs either by fixed-wing or by helicopter. Well, to make a long story longer, I had a great time from a great host, caught lots of large fish, and saw my comet, which was less than awe-inspiring because it was the worst appearance in two thousand years. We caught a lot of large fish, and I soon learned the art of stalking big fish in gin clear water.

One of the interesting things that happened there was a group of Japanese fishermen from Tokyo that came to Dick's lodge. The fishermen were very cordial and friendly. They all woke up about an hour or so before breakfast and went with their rods to the lawn between the lodge and the mountains. They were practicing casting. They were good. Their loops were tight, and they looked hot.

Our Japanese fly fishermen

The sad thing occurred after they got back from fishing for the day. Nobody had caught a fish. Somebody said that they loved to fish but didn't know how to fish. Where they came from in Japan, there were no rivers where they could really learn. They were, however, excellent casters.

Dick told us that it was important to hold your rod backward while walking because the glint of sunlight on a rod would put the fish down. One time, Dick was guiding me, and we stalked and fished to a log for about twenty minutes until we decided that no fish that large could possibly be so still for so long. We had a good laugh over that.

Dick ran the lodge as a lodge should be run. He had an open bar, lots of good food, great accommodations, and good guides. One of the things I remember best about the lodge is the question of hats. Well, Dick did hats right. He gave us a Cedar Safari cap as soon as we arrived. It always amazes me that you can spend thousands of dollars and travel thousands of miles to arrive at a remote camp, and then the outfitter tries to sell you a cheap souvenir baseball hat for $20. Hell, raise the price of the trip a little bit but give the client the damn hat for free. Make them feel good. Dick did it right, and it makes you want to go back. In fact, I went back in 2004.

Anyway, back to the boob job. At that time, I was married to my second wife, who was mammary challenged. That is to say that she had minimal boobs. That should have been my first clue. Anyway, she and I had agreed to meet in the Fiji islands for a few days of R and R on my trip back from New Zealand. As I got off the plane, I noticed that she didn't seem to be quite as flat as she had been before. She said, "How do you like them? If you can spend $3,500 to go fishing in New Zealand, I can spend $3,500 to get a boob job." That was a tough one to argue as I had had a great trip, and I had always wondered what it must be like to be a woman to go through life with meaningless boobs for men to stare at. At that time, I really didn't have the $3,500 to go fishing in New Zealand, and we didn't really have the $3,500 for a boob job, but who was I to argue about large breasts.

A Fisherman's Logbook
New Zealand, 1986

3/21/'86

Hunter River, New Zealand (inlet to Lake Hawea), glacial moraine
At 1:00 to 3:00 p.m., two fish caught, 4–5 pounds (one rainbow, one
  brown, black nymph, Adams, Br off another bow and brown,
  weather cloudy, water clear ad turquoise, windy)
Stewart Robertson (guide)
RD2 Sandymount
Dunedin, New Zealand
Fixed-wing flyout

3/22/'86

Young River, a tributary to Wanaka
11-1 O'clock caught 2 fish, 3-8.5 pounds, no hatches, 14 Adams
Dry fly, crystal clear
3-4 O'clock caught 2 fish 3-3.5 pounds, rainbows, no hatches, dry
  crystal clear, big old brown fly (in the box for 20 years—Stewart
  liked it.)
Missed three fish through early hooking, lost a brown nymph in one
  absolutely gorgeous day, no wind, not too hot, the three-fourths
  moon rising over the snowcapped peak in the evening, didn't
  see a lot of fish, however, the percentage hooked was high (Dad
  would have loved it)
Stewart and I walked in.

3/23/'86
Glacial Wilkin, Siberia

Wilkin 1030 O'clock—1- 3.5 lbs. RB 14 Adams, Dry, 2nd case, cold 1200 1-6 lbs., brown, brown nymph wet, ran 60 yards. Wrapped on rock and gonzo.

Siberia 300 O'clock--1-4 lbs., RB Nymph, Beautiful fish,

330 O'clock 1 4lb RB Nymph, good fish

Pretty Day, Partly Cloudy, some wind and no rain.

Helicopter fly out

3/24/'86

Dingle River—Stone Creek

At 11: 00 a.m., 1–3 pounds RB 14 Adams

At 12:30 p.m., 1–3.5 pounds RB, Chris R's hopper

At 3:00 p.m., 1–3 pounds RB stone fly, wet

At 4:00 p.m., 1–3 pounds RB Chris R's hopper

Heavy wind, clear, tough airplane hike, fished with Mac Butcher and Dick Frazier

3/25/'86

Upper Hunter

At 11:00 a.m., 1–5 pounds brown Chris R's hopper

At 3:00 p.m.,1–4.5 pounds RB Royal Wulff

At 3:30 p.m., 1–4.5 pounds RB Royal Wulff

At 4:00 p.m., 1–3.5 pounds Royal Wulff

Frazier had us casting to a log for twenty minutes. Stalking fish was fun. Two of Dick's knots came out while I was playing fish. He was greatly embarrassed.

3/26/'86

Upper Dingle, helicopter, one helluva ride, dropped 3,500 feet in thirty-five seconds

At 10:00 a.m., 1–3 pounds RB Royal Wulff

At 11:30 a.m., 1–3.5 pounds RB hopper

At 10:00 a.m., 1–4 pounds RB Royal Wulff

At 1:30 p.m., 1–5.5 pounds RB hopper—beautiful fish, took me downstream three hundred yards

At 2:30 p.m., 1–3.5 pounds RB Wulff

At 4:00 p.m., 1–4 pounds RB hopper

At 4:30 p.m., 1–3.5 RB Wulff

Terrible sand flies

South wind changed to north wind about 11:30 a.m., fished lots of pocket water, never buy weighted nymphs

3/27/'86

Clutha River (by car)

At 10:00 a.m., 1–4 pounds, RB mayfly nymph, fish got into backing into heavy water

This was underneath Hawea and was one of Stewart's favorites. He liked to fish it at night by sound. It rained like hell last night—windy as can be. So windy, it set off the stall alarm in the airplane.

3/29/'86

Morning, zero, blown off the lake, saw three to six fish

Afternoon, we walked up the Young.

At 3:00 p.m., 1–3 pounds RB Royal Humpy

At 5:20 p.m., 1–4 pounds RB #12 mayfly nymph

Walked a long way

Wanaka and Young River

New Zealand II

My second trip to New Zealand took place in 2004, and I went with Tom Parry, an excellent nymph fisherman. I've inserted longitude and latitude coordinates into this narrative in order to make it a bit more interesting for those who love cartography.

New Zealand, 2/20/'04
37 23.997 S
175 08.037 E
115 ft

On Thursday, we had a nice visit with Janet and John Free at their home in TeKawahta, New Zealand, about 50 miles south of Auckland. Janet and I were classmates in high school, and I'm one of the only ones to ever visit her. They have a chestnut farm in the middle of the wine country.

Janet and John Free

Friday, Lake Rotorua
S 38 08.664 S, 176 14.506 E
944 feet

Tom and I left Janet and John this morning and drove 75 miles south, where we fished for several hours.

We had breakfast at a little café where a waitress named Jane waited on us. She must have been eighteen to nineteen, married, and was very notable for the color of her eyes, which was a very pale blue, almost aquamarine.

When we got to the river, we had driven through several rainstorms, so we dressed for the worst—good thing we did as it rained on us several times. After fishing, we drove to Rotorua, which is built on the site of an old Volcano. As you walk about, you could smell sulfur, so we decided to stay at "Ann's Volcano Motel." We had a great dinner at Herb's.

We were still very worried about Janet's situation. Her son-in-law, Tony, was very sick with a dangerous tumor around his duodenum. They couldn't seem to get a straight answer from the docs as to whether it was malignant or not.

Yesterday, they said they found another mass in his testicles, very bad news, if true. Janet and John were not happy and seemed very distracted last night. They were going to operate on him Tuesday next, and we would know more by then. It didn't sound good. He was thirty-three and had a nine-month-old boy. He was half Maori, and his extended family had come from as far away as Australia to be with him. Janet's daughter, Jean Marie, was being very strong but must be very worried. I'll write more later.

Tom and I caught about thirty fish today with the largest about 18 inches, all rainbows. The water was a bit discolored but fishable. We caught some on a small humpy, but most took a nymph.

We had a bit of a scare when I waded out and sank to my crotch in soft mud. In fact, I couldn't get out by myself, and fortunately, Tom was nearby and was able to help me get out. If he hadn't been there, I would have been there for a long time. It was like quicksand.

We were at the motel now, watching cricket, which neither of us understands. We were going to fish the Rantotaukee tomorrow.

Saturday, 2/22/'04
38 41.485 S
176 04.455 E
1,198 feet
Taupo

We began this morning in Rotorua, the Sulphur City, and drove down toward Matarua on Highway 38. Most of the rivers were blown out as we were there during a one-hundred-year flood, and we fished for less than an hour without any luck. Poor us. It turned out that this was the rainiest February in one hundred years.

We got back into the car and had a nice drive to Taupo, where we had a great Thai dinner, and stayed in the Swiss Chalet Motel, which had nice rooms. I fixed a 220 DC, I think, light bulb. The country was 220 volts, which meant a transformer was necessary to charge the camera. Tom said I still snore. Bummer.

Hotel California, 2/22/'04
Our guide was Paddy Clark—Mangaone River
39 21.327 S
176 41.177 E
928 feet

Fishing was tough for me today. I caught five fish to 15 inches. Tom caught one 24 inches rainbow, which was a very nice fish. Weather was okay but one helluva hike down to the river from the car and a long way back.

Paddy named his lodge Hotel California, 2/23/'04.

In Eks River, we had good fishing. The weather was good, and the water was clear. We must have hooked eighteen fish, probably landed twelve. I caught the first brown, but the big one got away. I had him on for a few minutes, but we never saw him. It dove into a deep dark hole, and who knows how he got off. Damn. Tom and I caught fish for fish. I fished the 5 wt again. Tom brought the wrong spool for his 8 wt and had to use my new Battenkill reel, which I never did get to fish.

Tuesday, 2/24/'04
Hotel California to Napier
Mangaone River

Paddy Clark was a good guide. He was amiable and knowledgeable. He took us to water that was fishable and given the fact that we were there under terrible weather conditions, described to us as a hundred-year flood, we did well. Tom landed eight today, and I landed five. Big today was about 22 inches.

I carried water and betadine today, which I didn't do before—dumb mistake.

The water today was murky but fishable, barely. Hopefully, the south island is much better. Paddy had a great piano story: 1) surplus from school, 2) putting it out in the wilderness by Parfinua, drawing attention, 3) playing it, 4) wise-ass kids shooting it up, 5) his friends helping to locate kids, and 6) kids arrested.

I'd fish with Paddy again.

30 28.688 S
176 52.898 E
0 elevation

Very worried about Tony and Janet and John. Today was the day of the operation.

Wednesday, 2/25/'04
Napier to Christchurch to Queenstown
Christchurch
43 29.339 S and 172 32.294 E
112 feet

Queenstown
45 01.745 S
168 40.582 E
1,113 feet

Dick Frazier's Cedar Lodge South Island

Second visit—we talked to Dick Frazier, and he'd pick us up at 6:30 a.m. to go fishing. He was still the wonderful gentleman I knew in 1986.

Thursday, 2/16/'04
We fished the hunter. It was the worst day, windy. I caught a dink and missed 2 fish.
44 15.270 S
169 12.425 E
971 feet

Friday
We fished the Macarora and took 5 fish, only 1 worth talking about, a goof grown. We saw few fish.

Saturday, 2/28/'04
We fished in pouring rain all day. We took 1–4 pounds of beautiful rainbow on the Young. We walked through primeval forests, right out of the lord of the rings. Tom got zipped for the third day in a row. He was discouraged. Fishing seemed to be much tougher than eighteen years ago—unsettled water.

Our guide turned out to be the fisherman that T. Rowe Price used in one of their famous commercials back in the US. You might remember the independent guy fishing in a boat trying on a fly. This day also, Tom, who liked to use a fanny pack to hold his fly boxes in an elastic kind of pocket, lost at least two boxes in the underbrush.

We went back to look for them but never found them—a tribute to the river gods. I had told him that I liked my old beat-up vest since it had at least good pockets.

Sunday, 2/29/'04

It was a rainy morning. In the afternoon, we helicoptered down to the confluence of the Macaroa and Lake Wanaka and fished a pond that was full of fish. Everyone caught fish. I got 3, 1 nice brown and a couple of RBows. Dick Frazier was trying his best to get us over fish in very poor weather conditions.

Monday, 3/1/'04

We fished the Dingle, which was a pretty fast-flowing stream that went into Lake Hawea. Tom caught five nice rainbows, and I caught four, including the biggest one of the day, about 4 pounds.

I was happy that my waders weren't leaking, but when I got home, my pants and socks were wet. Sweat or water, I don't know. We tried to find the hole but couldn't, so sweat it was. One fish hit my fly 5 times, and I missed all five.

Tuesday, Upper Young
Hunter/Kyle, 3/3/'04
1–3 pounds rainbow
Tom caught a nice 5.5 pounds brown and missed a lot of fish.

Tom Parry

It was very sandy but cold and clear. I saw the stars for the first time really. I saw the LMC, Crux, and a strange beam of light from the NW. I didn't know what it was.

Auckland, 3/4/04

Dad's been gone twenty years Today. I miss him a lot. He would have loved to fish like this, but back then, we had no money.

We traveled to Queenstown and then on to Auckland. I think we overpaid Dick $1,000 apiece. We later got it back when Dick checked his books. We were dumb for not closely checking his verbal math. It was a great trip, even with the weather.

On the way to Queenstown, we had to stop and take the pictures above. They had strange customs with roadside fences. People hung their underwear, pants, and bras on the barbed wire, very funny stuff.

Auckland
36 38.296 S
174 47.177 E
46 feet

The devastation from the floods was easy to see from the air. It was truly a hundred-year flood.

The Pink Mouse Caper

Dave Oke and I had won a day's fishing at a place called Mt. Lassen Trout. It was the middle of April and California, was in full bloom with lots of wildflowers and tons of green grass. Mt. Lassen Trout touted itself as the home of monster trout, and Dave and I were ready. We went up into the foothills of the sierras and arrived early in the morning while the frost was still on the ground. We met the owner, and he pointed us in the direction of two very large ponds that looked like small dams. He said that they both had lots of large trout, and we should practice catch and release. We allowed as how that wouldn't be a problem, and with great expectations, we started to fish in the lower pond. We fished down there for a couple of hours and didn't do squat. So much for hungry and huge Mt. Lassen Trout.

Since fishing sucked, we admired the flowers and the birds. There were hawks, blackbirds, ravens, and vultures. After a while, a bald eagle settled into a tree across the lake. "A sign from heaven!" I shouted. It meant that we were going to catch fish but not in this pond. We must go to higher water. The pond was large and about 100 feet. From the front berm, there was a hazard in the form of branches, lilies, and moss. Dave, as he is sometimes, was futzing with his rod, line, and reel.

"Hey," I said, "no wonder you're a crappy fisherman. You can't get your line into the water, and you can't catch fish with your fly in the box." We opened the bottle of Jack Daniel's, as it was approaching 10:30 a.m. and had a drink to good luck and good fishing. I tied on a black leech pattern and plunked it out near the edge of the "stuff." I let it sink for a couple of seconds, and *bam*, I had a fish on. It played well, and when I beached him, he weighed about 8 pounds.

"Hey, Dave, I think I found the fish!" I shouted. Dave O said something unprintable and continued futzing. I immediately had another and larger fish on. "Oh, look how big this guy is! What a great fighter! What a humongous whale! Oh, this is wonderful," I shouted at the top of my lungs. Of course, all this was done for Dave's benefit, and he totally hated it when I was catching fish, and he was still futzing. After I landed and let the fish go, Dave announced that he was ready and walked over and started to fish.

We were facing east, looking directly at the snowcapped peak of Mt. Lassen, which erupted during the 1920s. In fact, my mother, as a little girl in Modoc County, in the northeast corner of California, remembered the smoke coming from the mountain. I'd climbed it a couple of times, and it was awesome to look down the throat of the volcano that erupted in such violence not so long ago.

Dave and I caught so many large fish over the next couple of hours that we were having too much fun if that is possible. We stopped briefly for a lunch of Jack Daniel's and potato chips and kept right on fishing. I don't know how many fish we caught, but the biggest was about 13 pounds. We discussed, briefly, that this might be considered a trout pond but soon cast that thought aside as we figured that we had to be great fishermen to catch this many trout, no matter where they were found.

About 2:00 p.m., the fish kind of went to sleep, so we did what came naturally. We had some more Jack Daniel's and got the lawn chairs from the van and sat down and looked for a while at the beautiful mountain and wonderful scenery. We fished for a while while we were sitting down. Fly-fishing from a sitting position was a new experience for both of us. They seemed to quit biting, and we sort of dozed off and tried different things. I tied a large dry fly, and a big trout hit it, and I told Dave that I was too tired to bring him in and asked him to do it for me. He obliged and said that I had always been a lazy dude. For about the next hour, nothing worked, and Dave decided that he'd get creative.

He looked around his tackle box and finally settled on a huge pink mouse and said that this was the fly. I said that a fish would have to be awfully stupid to hit a thing like that, and he said that this was his secret weapon and that a mouse this size was the perfect fly for these conditions. After another couple sips of John Daniel's, I said that just maybe a fish would hit it. Dave threw it out near the weeds and twitched it. Nothing happened, and I laughed and said that I told him so. He twitched it again, and a huge trout exploded out of the water and *missed* the fly. Dave twitched it again, and the same thing happened.

"Stupid fish!" I yelled, but by now, I was interested in his progress. Anther twitch and the fish was on. Dave played him masterfully into the trees off to our right where the trout got caught with this huge pink mouse prominently displayed on his lip. By now, Dave O and I were laughing our butts off and lamenting the fact that this fish was so stupid to take a pink mouse and so stupid to get caught in the brush. After a lot of pushing, pulling, rolling, and struggling, Dave O managed to break the fish off, and our last sight of this behemoth was it porpoising off through water with this unbelievable pink fluff hanging off of this lip.

We drank some more, sat some more, slept some more, and caught a couple of more fish. Finally, it began to get cold, and we decided that we had had a super day and deserved a good dinner where we discussed our poor pink mouse. We felt sorry for ourselves that we didn't have another one in our boxes and hoped that it would fall out of the trout's mouth before it scared the hell out of too many of his friends in the super pond called Mt. Lassen Trout.

Costa Rican Adventure

Who knows where ideas for great fishing trips come from?

At some point, I decided that I wanted to go fly-fishing for giant sailfish off the coast of Costa Rica, so when the opportunity came to book a trip, I took it.

My destination was Crocodile Lodge in the little town of Puerto Jimenez on the Osa Peninsula, on the Pacific side of Costa Rica. Everything started out just fine. On the day I left, I got up early, turned on the fishing shows, and wouldn't you know it, the program was Walker's Cay, and the topic was fly-fishing for sailfish in Costa Rica. Talk about karma!

I got to the airport on time, got to the gate on time, got on the plane on time, and the plane pulled away from the dock on time. We moved back about 50 yards, and the pilot cut the motor. Thunderstorms in Dallas delayed our departure by about an hour and a half. Since my connection to San Jose, Costa Rica, was only about an hour, I asked if I was going to be able to make the connection. "Oh yes, no problem," I was told. "In a situation like this, the whole system is simply backed up a bit."

Yes, the check was in the mail, and the south would rise again. When I got to Dallas, my flight had left on time, and I had to stay, at the airline's expense, at some hotel. Remember when the airlines used to do that. I got up early and caught the first flight out to Costa Rica. I expected to be met, like you usually are, by a representative of the travel company, but as it was Easter Sunday, there was no one to be found. Later on, I found out that *de costumbre* (as usual), when they realized that I wasn't on the intended flight, they had called and didn't know or couldn't figure out where I was. Would it have occurred to them to check the flight on the following day?

Anyhow, my Peace Corps experience took over, and I managed to hook up with a hustler named Luis, who turned out to be immensely helpful. He first tried to get me on a local commuter flight to Pt. Jimenez, but they were all full. As an ace in the hole, he booked me a space on a bus to Golfito, across the bay from Pt. Jimenez. When we couldn't get a flight, we headed for the bus terminal. I had all my suitcases, all my stuff, and was fully loaded down. The bus cost about $6 and took about eight hours to get there. The good news was that I felt like I was thirty-five years younger and back in the Peace Corps again. At least the roads were paved.

I got to Golfito, across the bay from Pt. Jimenez, about midnight and began looking for a hotel. I finally hailed a cab, and he said that there were two hotels in town, one for $4 a night and one for $3 a night. Of course, I took the $3 a night hotel. Hot, noisy, dirty, buggy—it had it all. I think it was a den of iniquity as you could hear sexual escapades going on as there were no walls but just separators.

I managed to find out where the boat was supposed to leave for Pt. Jimenez and was at the dock about 4:30 a.m. Of course, there was the standard guard who was still drinking with his buddies, a couple of whom were passed out on the pier. He said not to worry, as a boat would be along shortly, but he wasn't sure when. We became good friends, and as it happens in Latin America, he offered me his bottle of rum. At about 6:30 a.m., no kidding, a boat came by with the head guide from Crocodile Lodge, and I got my ride across the bay. It was a beautiful morning. I got to the lodge in time for breakfast and a drink with an umbrella in it. I met Dave Oke, and we and got to the boat in time for the 8:00 a.m. departure.

Our Guide

I don't know how it happened, but we found ourselves on four different boats on the first four days, and each boat managed to break down. The Costa Ricans were okay to fish with, but they weren't fly fishermen. They'd work a couple of hours trying to tease the sails in close enough to throw a fly at them then give up and try to fish with the big hardware. I don't know how many sails we took this way, but there were many. It was so cool to motor around, looking for sails as the ocean was beautiful. Several times we found ourselves invaded by thousands of dolphins swimming by. A curious thing about these is that some of them would periodically jump, whirl around, and crash back to the water.

Amazing!

Finally, after four days, we talked to the Jefe (Big Guy) and told him what we wanted to do. "Okay," he said and hooked us up with Todd, an expatriate who had probably been living on botanicals for several years. However, we liked him, and he said that he was going to get us a fish on flies or die trying.

After several hours of trolling with teasers, we succeeded in bringing several sails to the back of the boat. What a sight to see. These magnificent fish congregated in the clear Pacific water, looking for bait right behind the boat and who were looking for the bait that had disappeared.

I was first up and hooked a large one using the sailfish fly, which was 6 to 8 inches long and pink. After an hour, I boated a 125 pounds sail. What a hoot! Dave then hooked a smaller one and boated it. Then we broke Todd's boat. For some reason, the motor froze up, and we were becalmed, just like the ancient mariner. There was only one thing to do, and that was to drink some beer, which we proceeded to do.

Then the fishing gods smiled on us. A huge dorado came cruising by, and Todd yelled, "Get that f——king fly in the water." Dave, who was closer to the rod than I, grabbed it and threw it into the water. *Plop*, and the rainbow-colored dorado turned on it and took it. We had never seen anything like it. This *huge* beautiful dorado took off, and we swear that it didn't touch the water for 300 yards. Todd later called it greyhounding. Dave gave me the pole because it was my turn, and I fought it for an hour and forty-five minutes. I thought that was very fair after the permit caper. Halfway through the epic fight, I felt something pop in my shoulder, which turned out to be a torn rotator cuff. It bothered me for a while and was finally fixed with a couple of cortisone shots. It was worth it.

I needed Dave to spell me for a beer or two, so we took turns bringing the monster in. We covered it with our shirts and kept it wet for a couple of hours while we were rescued and towed in. The Costa Ricans couldn't believe that we'd taken it on a fly. When we got to the dock, it weighed in at 56 pounds.

The best I've been able to determine was that it was close to the world record for dorado on a fly. It wouldn't have counted any as there were two of us that handled the rod, and the line wasn't measured.

Oh, while I was fighting this dorado, Dave caught another with conventional gear when we floated by some stuff. It seemed like anywhere there was some flotsam floating around. It attracted baitfish, which then attracted the bigger fish. I think that if I were working some fishing boats, I'd put a large sea anchor on a raft of some sort and let the thing attract the bigger fish.

When we returned to the dock, we were practically famous. We weighed the fish, photographed it, and cleaned it. It dressed out so much meat that we fed the entire hotel. This lodge was wonderful. We had an open bar, and we drank a lot of the local stuff, as it was free to us. As in Colombia, one never drinks the *ultimo trago* (last drink) but always the *penultimo* (next to last) as the *ultimo* (last) is the one you drink just before you die. The word in Costa Rica was *el sarpe*. It meant the same and made you just as drunk.

We fished for a couple more days, but the fishing god had given us the fish of a lifetime. We took several more sails on flies but never again had a shot at such a large dorado, at least in this lifetime. Would I go back? You betcha!

Lee Arbuckle

A couple of years later, during a reunion of my Peace Corps group, I had a conversation with Lee Arbuckle, a graduate of Dartmouth, a rancher in Montana, and a very brilliant man, who had had MS for over thirty years. He said that if I ever found a place where he could fish and not have to walk much, he'd love to go with me. After thinking about things for a while, I decided that the best place we could go would be to go back to Costa Rica. It would be difficult for him to hike a river, but it would be easy to ride around in a boat catching fish. It was wonderful to see the expression on his face when he caught his first big sail. It was worth the trip. He's gone now, and I miss him.

Our guide and Lee Arbuckle

Jerry, Floribeth, and Lee

On this trip, I boated a 140-pound sail on a fly and had a great time with Lee. As he and I both spoke Spanish, we could talk with everyone. He spent a couple of days with a friend of his from his days in Bolivia when we returned to San Jose, Costa Rica. This was an extremely successful trip.

Guatemala and Hats for Children

Some years ago, and I don't remember when, on one of my trips to fish in the third world, I decided that there were a lot of children who had no access to head coverings. These children had no hats and would likely grow up to become victims of several forms of skin cancer, namely squamous and basal cell carcinomas. As they probably had no real ability to see dermatologists, they would undoubtedly become victims of disfigurement or other results of untreated skin cancer.

So I guess some of my Peace Corps bona fides got up from the past, and I decided to do something to help minimize the risk to these youngsters. Back in the day, management at our firm was always giving away baseball hats to all the people around me in the office. So every time I was going to go fishing in the tropics, I'd send around a memo asking my coworkers to search their closets and homes for surplus hats of any kind. I'd usually collect between thirty to fifty hats that I could pack in my go bag and take with me.

I took hats to Costa Rica, the Bahamas, Guatemala, Russia, Christmas Island, Mongolia, and Bolivia. The kids loved them.

I tried not to be the ugly American, and I'm hopeful that we were able to prevent some cancers from forming.

On one of my trips to Guatemala, we had a good time going to one of the poorer barrios (neighborhoods), and after we talked around a bit, the kids began to show up, and we were pressed to make sure the little ones got their share.

We were there to catch sailfish on flies, and we had good success. Archie Adams, Rufous Williams, Bob Mueller, and I had a good boat and a good captain. We decided that everyone could fish until they got a sail. We had three days for four people.

Archie Adams got a good sail

Archie, by the way, is a world-class fisherman and flytier. For this trip, he invented "the pink fly." This fly had caught sails in Costa Rica, Christmas Island for our circle of friends, including an incredible double on two 150 pounds plus sails by his wife Barbara Adams and Bob's wife Susan Mueller.

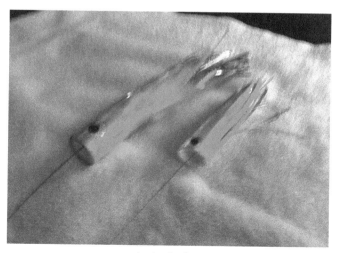

Archie's flies

Then Rufous Williams got his.

Bob Mueller got his

The fishing was not fast and furious. Being the gentleman that I am, I drew the short straw and was the last fisherman among equals. I didn't get up to bat until about 1:00 p.m. on the last day. We were going to fish until about 4:00 p.m. I began to get nervous. At 2:00

p.m., I was really nervous. At 3:00 p.m., I had to have more beer. About 3:30 p.m., we got into the sails again, and I threw the fly. One lovely fish took it, and the fight was on. I kept praying that he wouldn't get off.

We had a great captain who, in addition to calling out the lats and longs on his radio, really knew how to run a boat. As the sail ran and jumped, he would back the boat toward the fish so that it was easier for us old guys to take up the line. In Costa Rica, at Crocodile Bay, the captains didn't do that, and the fight lasted a lot longer and tired both the fish and the fisherman a lot more.

Finally, I brought the sail up and took pictures.

I always try to take a photo with the fly rod in my mouth to show that I indeed caught the fish on flies.

This was a great trip with good buddies. The next year we tried to go back, the operation jacked up the price to almost double, and we decided to pass.

The Land of Genghis Khan

Why would you travel halfway around the world to one of the remotest parts of the globe to fish waters that belong to one of the most ancient lands in the history of mankind? *Taimen*, that's why.

Taimen are a member of the salmonid family and grow to enormous sizes. What makes them especially interesting is that they rise readily to mouse patterns that are called verminators, fished dry.

Our goal was to catch one in the forty- to forty-five-inch range, which would probably weigh in at about 20–25 pounds. I didn't want to go alone, and the only friend I could find who wanted to make the trip with me was Chris Reidel of Christmas Island fame. It was a very long trip. I don't remember how many hours it took to get to Ulan Bator, the capital of Mongolia, but it was a long trek. Fortunately, I was able to fly first class going and business class coming back. I left Los Angeles and stopped in Seoul, South Korea, where I caught a KAL flight for another three and a half hours. I flew through Seoul, and Chris went through Beijing with a case of chardonnay. After we landed and got together, we were met by a young Mongolian who spoke perfect English and worked for Frontiers, our outfitter. We got to our hotel, where we began to settle in. What an interesting place. I call it a thirty-foot city, where the buildings look great until you get closer than 30 feet, and then you can see all the cracks left by the communist builders. Mongolia was freed about 1990 and is making some strides toward democracy.

We toured the city, visited Buddhist shrines, and I was able to purchase some really neat hats and camel-hair vests. We went out on a tour of the countryside, looking for Khan's Karakorum, and one of the first things you notice is that there are no fences and a lot of nomadic-looking people. We learned that what we called yurts are really named gers, and what we didn't know was that we would be living in one for a week when we got to the fishing camp.

The Eg River and our gers

We stayed in the capital for a day and a half, and then we got on a Russian helicopter for a four-hour ride to our camp.

Jerry Estruth

There were approximately twenty fishermen who were going to be split up among three camps. We flew over beautiful rolling plains without any houses, farms, or fences. We saw a lot of gers.

Mongolia Jerry Estruth

We stopped at an extremely remote airfield after about two hours to refuel. We decided that the guy stationed there must have really pissed someone off to get that job. I mean, it was nowhere.

Then we took off again and headed into the hilly country of Northern Mongolia. The helicopter was so loud that I was happy I had brought along my earmuffs that I used for target practice.

After another two hours, we arrived at the camp, which consisted of five gers nestled between a ridge of hills and a huge river. This was to be our home for the next week. Chris and I got the ger on the end of the row, farthest away from the cookhouse and a short walk to the showers and the crappers. The showers were heated by a wood-fired cookstove, a style that I encountered in Colombia. The porta-potties were lighted and lined with Astroturf, a very nice combination. We had our orientation and hopped into the boats and tried out afternoon fishing. All we caught that first afternoon were a couple of lennock, a very primitive trout. We didn't see any taimen. When we got back to the camp, we went outside to sit at some of the tables alongside the river, where we sampled our Genghis Khan vodka. There were two men already seated there, and we soon learned that they were very cool Stanford types, father and son, named Kaufman. They liked to play cribbage, so we were able to play almost every night before dinner while we sampled vodka and some wonderful wine that Chris had carried across the ocean and through Beijing.

Playing cribbage and talking

It was cold and got colder. The first night, we had a folkloric concert by a family of Mongolians. They played several different instruments, the most notable of which was the horse-headed fiddle. The music was very melodic, and all the songs told a story. They talked about brave nomads and the mother waters.

Our camp was on the Eg River, about halfway between Lake Houvsgul and Lake Baikal. We were told that this lake and river system contains about 25 percent of the fresh water in the world. The rivers would freeze solid by the second week of October, and we were there in the third week of September. I think if I went back again, I'd go in August because the water would be warmer, and I think the taimen would be more active.

For us, the fishing was slow, okay, but slow. We heard about a guy from Indianapolis, who came back every year in the second week of August. We might have been a little late, but it was wonderful. We could hear Elk bugling in the hills during the day and wolves howling at night. The Kaufmans would go hunting in the mornings and go fishing in the afternoon. We had wonderful wild birds to eat every night. The Kaufmans called it "casting and blasting."

Chris and I fished hard every day. We kept catching taimen about 33–35 inches long—okay but not what we came for. It was fun as these fish would come clear out of the water to take these mice patterns or verminators. We caught a number of lennock and taimen until the last day when our guide pulled in to an eddy and asked which one of us would like to fish there. We kind of mentally flipped a coin, and I got off to fish this big eddy. Chris went up a few hundred yards to another eddy where he proceeded to catch a 42 inche taimen.

Chris Reidel and our guide and a forty-five-pound taimen

He thought it was wonderful that, as he put it, "one of the shittiest fishermen in the world skunked one of the best in the world." There is a wonderful picture of me looking totally pissed off and Chris beaming from ear to ear.

We passed a wonderful week of great weather. The stars were fabulous, the food great, the wine and vodka superb, and the beds were very comfy. I was the designated fire builder and would get up two or three times a night to make a new fire. The larch would burn fast, but we were comfortable. Sandra Day O'Connor, the Supreme Court justice, had fished this same water the previous week.

One of the most memorable things about the trip happened every night when it was very quiet. You could hear the river moving rocks along the riverbed. It sounded like a subtle rustling of paper. You could hear the rocks sliding over each other in the river. It was a soft, mesmerizing, rustling sound.

Spatsizi, Canada
The Land of the Red Goat

A couple of years ago, I was fishing on Russia's Kamchatka Peninsula with my friend and a very good fisherman from Kansas named Archie Adams. I've written about Archie before, but during this trip, he said that I had to take my son Thomas to a place called Spatsizi if I wanted him to catch a lot of fish. It took two years of procrastination, but we finally made it, along with Joe Decker, his son Robby, Jake Iantosca, and Jeff Wilkes of frigate bird fame.

Our group

On Thursday, 8/9/'07, we left Smithers, British Columbia, aboard a de Havilland Otter and headed north. We didn't really know what to expect, but all our expectations were exceeded. At this latitude, it was still light very late (54 20.168 N and 127 56.460 W, sunrise 553, and sunset 914). After flying for an hour and a half over some of the prettiest glaciers and mountains you have ever seen, we arrived at the lodge on Lake Laslui (57 20.168 N, 127 56.469 W, elevation 4,116 feet, sunrise 547, and sunset about 1100).

The lodge

We had lunch and went fishing. The cabins were nice and warm, the crapper was small, and the shower was neat and tidy. They said we could drink the water anywhere without treatment. It must be one of the few places left in the world that had pure water.

After lunch, Thomas and I flew out in a floatplane with Tim and went to Duti Lake. Tim said a prayer before we took off, which made us all feel better, and Thomas sat in the copilot's seat. It turned out later that Tim had been part of pilots for missions and spent two years flying missionaries, doctors, and supplies around Africa. Tim showed Thomas what all the controls meant and let him turn a few knobs, dials, and levers.

08/12/2007

Tim's plane

Duti Lake was beautiful, and while I was futzing with equipment, Thomas was in the water catching fish.

Thomas

Between the two of us, we must have caught about a hundred trout between 12–16 inches. Then a loon appeared. I love loons and the haunting sounds they make. It started to rain and hail, and fishing slowed down a lot. Tim took a fish and fileted it out and cooked it over an open fire for lunch. It was delicious.

We flew back under a lowering ceiling and saw a couple of moose in some little lakes. Thomas and I built a wood fire in the cabin and dried out. We had a nice dinner and went to bed before it got dark. I was writing this about six in the morning on Friday. Thomas and the guys were still asleep. I was in the main lodge overlooking the lake that was covered by low clouds. There was no wind, and the surface of the lake was as smooth as glass. I built a fire for warmth while I was waiting for the kitchen workers to get some coffee made.

The big news on Friday was that Thomas caught more fish than his dad. Thomas caught a 6-pound bull trout and several beautiful rainbows. Between the two of us, we must have nailed seventy-five fish. For lunch, we fried a trout over an open fire. The fish was cooked with garlic and butter and was excellent. Thomas fished very well, and his casts looked great.

On Saturday, I fished with Jeff, and we had a super day. We caught bigger fish. We took them on nymphs, dries, buggers, and my super Steve's woven sparkle of South American fame. Carrie cooked us a trout for lunch, and we had a visit from a very small semipalmated sandpiper. Armand, the quiet one, was the pilot in the green plane, which was made in Poland. We were at Stalk Lake. We also saw a huge, beautiful bald eagle.

08/15/2007

Bald eagle

Thomas fished with Jake and did well. He caught another bull trout on a dry fly, one of the few people ever to do so. They, too, caught a bunch. Stalk Lake was 57 06.147 N, 127 35.609 W, 4,448 feet high.

Sunday morning at the lodge—it was a beautiful sunrise with reds, yellows, and a clear sky. This was the first day that it had been clear at dawn.

08/12/2007

Up to now, we had "scud" or low-lying fog that we had to wait to burn off before we could fly. The weather had been fairly good but with periods of rain, wind, and hail. One day, we even heard thunder, but they said that was rare.

The land was incredible. There were lots of green and lots of water, lakes, streams, ponds, snow, and rock. The contrasts were starling, and we were lucky we'd been able to fly over it. The lodge was first class. The food was great.

Thomas raved about last night's creamy leek soup with bacon. We had coffee at 6:30 a.m. and Thomas's fave of French toast and cereal. He even ate Canadian bacon. Goose down quilts kept us toasty warm in the cabins. It was hard to keep the firs in the woodstove from getting us too hot. As I wrote this, there was a little fog blowing gently across the lake.

We flew over a reddish-colored mountain called "Spatsizi," which meant "Land of the Red Goat" in some native American tongue. It was a mountain of iron oxide, and the goats liked to roll in it for some reason, making their coats red.

Yesterday at the stalk, we saw a beautiful bald eagle come fairly close and pick something off the beach about 200 yards away.

On Sunday, Thomas was tired and didn't fish much. We went to stalk/sheep outlet into Kitchener Lake, 57 03.797 N, 127 29.786 W, 4,305 feet high. It was gorgeous! Without moving very much, we must have caught seventy-five fish before and after lunch. Then we motored across the lake to Loser Creek and caught a bunch more. Twofers, or doubles, were common.

Thomas rallied and caught some. The fish loved my Steve's Sparkle Pupa, the horsefly. Then I found a shiny flashaboo green and yellow bugger and fished that forever until I lost it in a fish.

Did I mention that we had creamy leek soup last night with bacon? Thomas was still raving about it. This morning, we had wonderful eggs benedict, and we weren't limited to two, so I had six.

(Thursday morning, 9/16/'07, Laslui SR 559, SS 911)

On Monday, Thomas and I fished rognass, a large river flowing out of Kitchener Lake, 57 02.590 N, and 127 20.859 W.

Fishing started slow, and then I changed to a green/chartreuse wooly bugger, and it got hot. I took a lot of fish at the outlet, and then we moved after lunch to the second big hole, and I must have taken fifty fish more. Thomas was getting discouraged as it was big water and hard to fish. Then we moved on to the third hole, and the sun came out. Hatch came on, and we put a dry fly on Thomas's line and put him in at the head of the hole, and he started to catch fish. Then he caught more fish, all on dries. There were fish jumping all around, and he had a field day. I think he learned how to hook, fight, and land large fish right then and there. It was perfect with the sun behind us. It was nice riffly water, and big trout were jumping all over.

About 5:00 p.m., we flew over to the amazing Firesteel to spend what turned out to be two nights with Ray Collingsworth, Carrie's father and one of the original pioneers to put Spatsizi together (57 01.866 N and 127 10.871 W).

This was a large, hugely prolific river with about four thousand fish per mile. Once again, as on Tuesday, my Steve's Sparkle Pupa did amazing things, and Thomas and I caught some seventy-five fish between us. Ray and his nephew, Mark, who was thirteen, were fun to fish with. We fished the "delta," which is harder to fish, and we still took seventy-five fish between us. Ray was one of the pioneers up here and started Spatsizi lodge. He was quite the character and had a lot of stories about wolves, bears, and the early days here. He told one story about how the crows manage to catch the mountain goats. He said that when they spot a goat on a ledge, several of them flew at the goat's head. Then they circled around the goat until the poor beast got dizzy and fell to his death. Then the birds ate the carcass.

He had his own special cabin, and Thomas and I had a cabin of our own that had a fussy stove. We had several discussions about whether or not we had to crack the door for ventilation.

On Wednesday, we fished upstream quite a long way. The boat had a 25 horsepower Yamaha, and as Ray had to fly out on some business, we fished with Billy Labonte, Carrie's husband, and Mark. At lunch, we hammered them on a dry fly. Then we went further upstream where Thomas got into them. It was so much fun to see him come into his own. I think the trip had been very good for him. We saw lots of wildlife. There was one moose that swam in front of the boat, and we got fairly close to him.

Once again, Steve's Pupa showed its worth, and I put it on and hammered them again. Then we started to float downstream, and Billy said we could fish from the boat. Thomas, after a while, got up in front and cast well off of both sides of the boat and took a bunch of fish. Billy said that the guys were jealous of us having two nights on the Firesteel, which, by the way, is a great name for a river. We decided to tell them that at first, it was because of our wit, charm, and good looks but decided that we'd tell them that Ray said we were the best fishermen he'd seen this year and invited us to stay over. In fact, he offered to comp us in for next week, but we had to decline because Thomas had to get back to school. They didn't believe us, but that was our story, and we were sticking to it.

We had dinner after Tim got us back at about 7:00 p.m. We saw a caribou from the plane. Dinner was wonderful as usual, and we all sat around a big campfire smoking "gars" and went to bed at about 10:30 p.m. Thomas stayed up till I don't know when, and he built a fire that heated the cabin up to 95 degrees. He was growing up. Those were good days.

08/15/2007

The length of daylight had diminished by twenty-seven minutes a day during the week we'd been there. Wow! At this rate, winter would set in soon. Billy said that global warming had made the winters warmer but thought it was a natural cycle. So did I, but greenhouse gases contribute, I thought.

We saw a bald eagle, a Birrell's goldeneye, and a lot of mergansers. Up there, they shot the mergansers because they had only recently been seen there, and they ate a lot of trout.

Today dawned bright and clear, just like yesterday. These were the first two days of the trip without clouds all day. On Tuesday, we didn't see the sun at all but escaped any rain. The bad news was that we had to go home today. The Otter would be here about 11:00 a.m. with a new crop of fishermen and would take us back to Smithers, where we'd stay the night, and on Friday, we'd fly to San Francisco and Phoenix and then drive a couple of hours to Tucson.

Kamchatka

The name alone creates visions of the Silk Road through ancient cities like Samarkand and Tashkent mixed in with journeys on the Orient Express. For fly-fishers, however, it had become a destination spot for catching huge rainbow trout on large dry flies.

Our trip began with a long journey from Tucson through Los Angeles on to Korea and then through Vladivostok and finally to Petropavlovsk, which is on the east coast of the Kamchatka peninsula on the Pacific coast of Siberia. We were about 52 degrees north and about seventeen hours ahead of Tucson.

Petro-Pavlovsk Airport

Lenin

We flew out one more hour on an ancient but reliable Russian helicopter to our destination river, the Karpushka (that means cabbage in Russian and is used to cover up its real name, the Savan).

Our Russian guides, cooks, and translators were waiting for us on the river, along with our American leader from Ouzel Expeditions in Anchorage, Todd Hibner.

Natasha, Jerry, and our translator, Tanya

We changed into our waders and started fishing while our hosts set up camp and rigged our Sotar rafts for our journey downriver. There were other outfitters in Kamchatka that established a base camp and then jet boat their guests up and down the river. That might be more comfortable, but I thought that with everyone in that camp fishing basically the same water, only on different days, our way was better because we were continually fishing new water by easily wading downstream each day to a new camp where we slept in comfortable tents each night. The water was big enough, and the bottoms were smooth enough that we were continually fishing without getting in the other guy's way.

The first day, the five of us fished egg-sucking leeches and caught a lot of the resident char between 20–25 inches long. You had to beat them off the leach to get to the rainbows. About noon, I decided to fish on top with mice and verminators. With these flies, I was able to eliminate the char, and I started to get into rainbows, which averaged 26 inches. Pretty soon, we all were "mousing." What a thrill to see them smash the floating mouse and then jump, jump, and jump again.

They looked like a rainbow-colored side of beef leaping out of the water. Each of us averaged ten to fifteen of these enormous trout a day. Although the trip fish caught by my good friend and excellent fisherman Archie Adams was 32 and ½ inches long, we all caught trout over 30 inches once or twice a day.

Archie and I had a great adventure, trying to catch a recalcitrant trout. We finally brought it to the net, and it was another fun occasion.

Jerry, Archie, and our guide, Todd Hibner

Jerry

Everyone used an 8 wt rod with an 8 or 9 floating wt forward line. We attached about 8 feet of 0X or simply a twenty-pound test leader as these fish were not leader shy. A cute, size 2, well-greased mouse was then attached, and if you could throw it accurately about 70–75 feet, you could take a bunch of fish. A lot of the fish were

106

taken near overhanging trees, bushes, rocks, and snags. You could bet that if there was a structure or deep water, a hog would hammer your mouse. The fish weighed a lot, and if they took the verminator near a snag, you had to horse them for a little bit until you got them into open and deeper water because they'd break you off in the bushes if you let them run back to their hiding places. By the way, a big net and a wading staff were helpful.

I developed a special technique to entice a strike and catch consistently above average fish. If you're interested and promise not to tell, I might share it with you.

The ten of us, all experienced and well traveled, got along well and were on the river for a week and enjoyed a simply wonderful trip and decided that there was no place in the world for such superb, healthy, and large rainbows, including New Zealand. There might be other places where the occasional fish might be bigger, but for consistency, you couldn't beat Kamchatka.

Dining tent

The Russians were great, and the food was super. Our Natasha was a super chef. She'd often gather wild mushrooms and make soups. Boy! Were they good! Volodya, Natasha's husband, Dimitri, and Tanya, our translator, formed the rest of the group, and they would cater to our every need. They were excellent.

You might remember the old saying that said, "You can't get there from here." Well, to and from was the worst part of the trip as it was long, tiresome, and boring. Two years ago, when I went, there was a four-hour flight from Anchorage to Petropavlovsk, which was fairly easy as you could overnight in Anchorage, get up early the next morning, and be fishing in Russia by that afternoon. That airline Magadan went belly up, so we had to go the long way around. The trip home was forty hours of traveling, but believe me, it was worth it. I'd be going back.

My third trip was in 2008, around the first week of August. Once again, our group was fine, and the fishing was wonderful. The biggest fish I caught was 33 inches, and Paul Allred, the outfitter, estimated that it weighed some 16–17 pounds. These trout got big because there was a lot of natural food in the water. They were born in the river, and after a couple of years, they went to the ocean and fattened up. They then returned to the river where they lived for the rest of their lives. They fed on mice, lemmings, and other aquatic creatures. One apocalyptic story recounted that one guide cut one big trout open and found five ducklings inside.

After lunch one day, I put on all my layers of clothing—pants, wader, rain jacket, wading belt, vest, hat, and camera. Not long down the river, I had to answer the call of nature, but before I could get unhooked and find a spot, the urge was unbelievable and very imminent. There was no tree to lean against, so I tried my best to get everything out of the way. I managed to get the toilet paper out of my back pocket, but I was unable to miss my waders. Lesson—don't crap in your waders. My good friend, Mike, was laughing his ass off. After washing my waders in the river, it wasn't too catastrophic but still was awful.

In the last two days of the trip, we were invaded by a huge and prolific run of salmon called "pinks" or "humpies." These were pretty colored fish and probably weighed between 8–12 pounds. What was incredible though was the quantity of them. They filled the river from bank to bank and from top to bottom. I've always heard that "there were so many salmon that you could walk across the river on their backs." Well, this time, it was true.

It bothered the trout, so our topwater fishing was trashed, and we should have switched to bigger egg-sucking leeches. The salmon chased the big trout out of their ordinary holding water, so we couldn't find them on top. It was a marvelous run, and it was only later that we figured out that we were fishing in the wrong place. We'd know better next time.

It was exciting to see the wildlife. We saw an amazing number of bears. One time, I fished around an island and came upon a mother and two cubs. I retreated immediately.

One of the special birds we saw was the Steller's sea eagle. I think it was native to Kamchatka or Eastern Siberia, and it was truly special. We saw it fly out of its nest, where we saw the heads of some eaglets.

Steller's sea eagle

Kamchatka is the home of about twenty-five active volcanoes. We flew over one, for some unknown reason, while it was erupting.

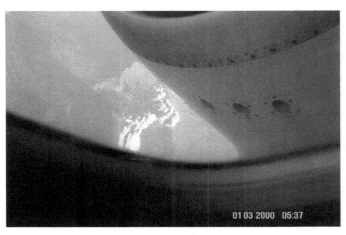

Erupting volcano

I'm going to enclose some other fotos of the beautiful mountains.

09/11/2007

Then I'll put in some travel log kind of fotos.

Red fox

Church

09/10/2007

Goodbye

Nick, Walleyes, and Northern Pike

When Nicholas was about fifteen, he and I were invited to go with our good friend, Dr. Joseph Decker, and his friends, Jake Iantosca and Dave to Lake Brisbois, about a two-hour flight north of Winnipeg, Canada, to fish for northern pike and walleyes. Since I had never fished for either and Nick had certainly not fished for them, we decided to go.

The flight was uneventful, and the floatplane put us down on a huge lake that was absolutely without any noticeable landmarks. Joe, knowing this, had suggested that I get a GPS system so I could find our way back to camp because being out on such a big lake with no landmarks, it would be very difficult to get back to our home cabin. So I bought a Magellan, and as it turned out, it was very useful and was really necessary to navigate around this huge lake.

The cabin was rustic and simple. There were no windows and no screens, so the mosquitoes this far north were plentiful, aggressive, and hungry. We had Coleman burn rings that did a reasonable job of keeping them away, and we had a great time.

We brought our fly rods and our spinning gear as we didn't have any real idea about what we were doing. So Nick and I grabbed the first motorboat and sped off to the inlet where we began to hammer the northerns.

We used spoons and lures and heavy tippet material with wire leaders as the northerns have very rough mouths. The pike were hungry as we were there in the first week in June, just after ice-out. We soon quit fishing with hardware and used our fly rods for the rest of the trip. The weather, although cold, was beautiful, and sunburn was a real problem. Nick had never seen such big and mean fish, and if the truth were known, neither had I. The pike were vicious and actually dangerous.

We had a big net to get them into the boat, and then we had a hell of a time getting the treble hooks out of their mouths. If we go back, I will cut off two of the three hooks and fish with a single hook with the barb mashed down. We handled the fish with glacier gloves so as not to get cut up from the sharp plates that they had in their mouths. A small pike was about 36 inches, and we caught them up to 45 inches. These were big mean fish, and they put up a good fight. Nick was ecstatic, and so was I.

We'd begin fishing at about 8:00 a.m., just after breakfast. Dave was a great cook and loved to do it, so we ate very well. About 10:00 a.m., after catching so many pike, we couldn't count them all, we'd pull up stakes and go over to the walleye hole. Honestly, there was one spot, about a twenty-five-minute motor from where we caught so many pike, where we'd catch so many walleye it was ridiculous.

We marked the honey holes on the GPS so we'd find them again and proceeded to have a lot of fun. These walleyes were the first that we'd ever caught and were beautiful fish. We'd keep about two apiece for lunch, and we'd let the rest go. We fished with smaller tackle for these as they were smaller, and it wasn't too long before we started to fly-fish for them. They were a tremendous amount of fun on the lighter tackle.

Then we'd go back to the cabin and have fresh walleye filets for lunch. Absolutely delicious! After a rest, we'd go back out to hammer the pike for the afternoon.

After the first day, we gathered in the cabin and took stock of how many fish we caught. We figured that we each had caught thirty fish in the morning and thirty fish in the afternoon. So each pair of us caught about 120 fish or 240–250 a day.

After I frightened Nick with some of my boating techniques, Nick took over the motor and learned how to get around. One time, I had a lot of fly line out, and we were trolling backward, trying to get a pike to hit a popper on the end of the line. Nick put the boat into a rock, and I fell on my ass. I was not happy and told him that he had to look backward to see where we were going. Actually, I was being a jerk and really out of line.

Anyway, we survived all that and proceeded to catch a ton of fish. Sometimes, we'd just drift along and lean back and cast and continue to catch fish. About every twenty minutes, a huge jet would fly overhead, leaving a long contrail, and we finally decided that they were on a route from Europe to the US on the great circle route.

Then there was the afternoon that we went to the secret spot—*bad idea*. It was a small lake, maybe just a pond that empties into Lake Brisbois. To get there, where we were told the really big ones were, we had to portage the boat over about 15 feet of roots, rocks, and other obstacles. We got into the other water and proceeded to flog the water, and we did pick up a couple of fish, but the big ones were either hiding or missing in action. Then what we hadn't thought about was that we had to reverse the process and drag the boat back over the inlet/outlet and get to the big lake. Man, that was a lot of work. I was very glad that Nick was big and strong.

At this time of year, it never really got dark, and the sun seemed to set about 10:00 or 11:00 a.m. and rise about 4:00 or 5:00 p.m. It was really always twilight, so we could watch out for bears as we trundled out to the outhouse where we'd regularly get out butts chewed on by mosquitoes.

At the beginning of the trip, Nick was very tentative when it came to fishing, but by the end, he was very intentional about catching all the fish that it was possible to catch. He had morphed into a very serious fisherman.

The end of the trip came all too soon as the floatplane came to pick us up. I told Nick that if he lived to be a hundred, he'd never again catch so many quality fish as we had caught this week. Between the four of us, we figured that we had caught and mostly released over 1,600 fish. It was an unbelievable trip, and I'd like to do it again with Nick.

Canadian Fishing Trip Version II

Lake Brisbois, Canada, 6/2/'01
We were at 56 degrees N and 100 degrees W at
a beautiful lake in Northern Canada.

It took almost two days of traveling to get there, and all the planes kept getting progressively smaller until the last little de Havilland Otter, a two-engine, eight-seater, floated down and landed on the little lake of about 20 square miles.

We were staying in a *rustic* cabin with propane heaters, stoves, lights, and refrigerators. Dave Schiff, Joe Decker, Nick Sgarlata, and I all had our own sleeping bags and bunks.

The first thing we did, of course, was get organized, then we went fishing.

The first afternoon, we must have caught, between the four of us, about fifty to sixty fish, on hardware, between us. I got a 9-pound northern pike, a really mean-looking fish.

The Magellan GPS system, while probably not totally necessary on the lake, was truly remarkable. With great accuracy, it got us home last night. I hardly needed to watch the shoreline. At midnight, last night, it was still light enough to see across the lake. Then the sun came up about 4:00 a.m. Fascinating.

Day 2, Sunday
Magellan worked great! We caught so many fish today that Nick and I went fly-fishing for northerns in the afternoon. We used wire leaders and red and white flies.

I used a 10 wt with a floating line. The biggest I got was 40 inches, and we estimated that it went 20 pounds.

Nick motored us around most of the day after he got over his fear. He was upset that he was losing equipment, and I said not to worry because that's why we bring so much stuff.

Nick and Dave got into walleyes in the afternoon, trolling with smaller red eyes.

We must have caught forty pike over 30 inches.

Wednesday morning

Perfect weather so far. Sunblock was the order of the day. Fishing was still good. I caught about twenty-five fish (pike) last night on poppers and streamers. Boy, were they vicious, very hard to deal with. I guess teenagers were hard to deal with. I'd found that I've gotten mad at Nick a few times because he treated me in a condescending manner. He had been, on the other hand, a big help around here. He loved to drive the boat, but he was sometimes careless.

Yesterday, he was backing it up and hit a rock. I was standing because I was fly-fishing. Well, the boat stopped, and I didn't. I fell backward and really hurt my back. Cracked rib? Torn muscle? I don't know, but it sure hurt.

Thursday noon

Nick and I went back to the walleye hole and caught another forty to sixty fish. We had 2–24 inches fish this morning. Dave Schiff had given us a two-way radio so we could check in with each other. Like most of those most things, they didn't work all the time, and I'd hate to depend on them if I had a real problem.

The guide brought us more gas and a new propane refrigerator. Dave was a great cook, and all in all, we were having a great time.

Friday morning—one more day

Weather had been warm and perfect. There was no rain or even a light wind. We thought it might be blowing up something last night as the cloud patterns changed. But, as usual, I worked my weather mojo on it, and today was beautiful. We woke up to the sound of Canadian geese in the marsh next to the cabin.

I read Dave Schiff's son-in-law John Greensfeld's account of summiting Denali. He didn't make the top at 13,000 feet as the weather was too extreme. He was an astronaut, and he spent thirty-eight days in space fixing the Hubble and the Space Station.

Fishing was superb.

Noon

Nick and I caught seventy-five to eighty walleyes in the walleye hole, and I got a twenty-four-inch, a three-and-three-fourth-pound one on a fly.

57 28.128 N
Long: 100 46.660 W
About 1,180 feet at the cabin

Aren't Ex-Wives Wonderful

I don't know who first said it, but it goes something like this, "No matter how wonderful you think she is, she is some other guy's worst nightmare." This new woman in my life, however, professed a great desire to fly-fish, so I asked myself, "Self, how bad can she be?" I said there were a few things she had to learn and showed her this from Carol Von Raesfeld:

HOW TO BE A GOOD FISHIN' BUDDY

by

Carol von Raesfeld, Fishmaster

March marks the season opener of Flycasters' monthly fishouts and, just as we must renew our fishing licenses each year and learn the new legislatively-imposed fishing regulations to prepare for the fishouts, we should also take some time to refresh our memory regarding fishing "rules of the road" which will enable each of us to be better fishing buddies. Here is a brief synopsis of basic stream etiquette--whether on an organized fishout or just out enjoying the sport on your own.

In years past, the dry fly fisherman fished exclusively upstream and his counterpart, the wet flyfisherman, downstream. Because of the skill level required, the difficulty encountered and out of respect to the dry flyfisherman, the wet flyfisherman was required to yield their stream to their approaching counterpart.

Today, with flyfishing methods so varied, stream etiquette is not as clear as it once was. Dry flyfishermen are often found fishing downstream and their wet flyfisherman counterparts fishing upstream. Consequently, certain rules and courtesies have developed which govern one's conduct on and about the stream. A knowledge of those rules and courtesies help the inexperienced, educate the ignorant and enhance the pleasures of flyfishing for all of us.

The first basic rule in flyfishing--as in all aspects of life--is The Golden Rule: DO UNTO OTHERS AS YOU WOULD HAVE THEM DO UNTO YOU. Sounds a little corny, but it's the one thing you should always remember.

RULES for WADING

Before entering a stream where another flyfisherman is casting, wait a few moments and observe the area of the water they are fishing and whether they are moving upstream, downstream or fishing in one place to rising fish.

If they are fishing downstream, enter the water upstream, allowing sufficient room so that you do not disturb the fish in the water they are fishing.

If they are fishing upstream, then enter downstream with the same consideration. If in doubt, speak quietly to the fisherman and inquire as to which area they are fishing and in what direction they are moving.

If you are wading and overtake a slower angler fishing in the same direction, get out of the water and walk around them. Go as far past them as reasonably possible before returning to the stream, preferably around a bend and out of sight.

When meeting another fisherman approaching from an opposite direction, ease around the edge of the stream behind them or get out, if possible, as you pass. It is perfectly alright to have pleasant conversation as long as you do not disturb any fish within their casting range.

Above all, one should remember that **sound travels approximately five times faster beneath the water's surface than above.** Thus, the turning over of rocks with one's feet, the kicking of gravel, the churning of mud/silt and the splashing of waders, not only spooks the fish in the immediate area, but often has a pyramiding effect on those fish 40 to 50 feet beyond the carelessly wading angler.

Many fly fishermen, wading with enthusiasm to join and converse with a friend or stranger in the stream, are met with coolness or antagonism because they have created a chain reaction which inadvertently has put down the fish to which an otherwise friendly angler had been presenting their fly. **WADE QUIETLY and CAREFULLY.**

RULES for CONVERSATION

While I am personally convinced that conversation between fisherman on or in a stream has a negligible effect, if any, upon the fish below, traditions dictate otherwise.

I find myself, as others do, speaking softly to my fellow anglers. I believe that while fly fishermen, myself included, would be well advised to consider and concern themselves with the underwater disturbance caused by wading and body movement in the stream environment, we tend to relate fish to our environment and make no attempt to acclimate ourselves to theirs.

In our environment, if we do not wish to disturb someone, we speak softly; however, since fish are not privy to our conversations, the emphasis is ill-placed. The solitude and concentration one often finds in flyfishing also contributes to the softly spoken words. Consequently, this tradition should be respected and honored by all. Speak only in a tone and with a volume necessary to be heard and softly understood by those with whom you are conversing.

RULES for COMMUNITY FISHING

Fishing for the anadromous fish (i.e., shad, steelhead and salmon)(and Flycasters' Pyramid Lake fishout, for another example) is sometimes a community affair. Fishermen will be lined up several feet apart to fish a stretch of holding water. Before wading into the line, make sure that there is room for you. If in doubt, wait to be invited or ask permission.

If you are taking an upstream position in the line, wade into the water about two feet farther than your downstream neighbor. This will prevent your retrieve from snagging them.

If you are taking a downstream position in the line, wade about two feet short of your upstream neighbor, so that they won't snag you!

RULES for BOATING OR FLOATING

Angling from a float tube or a boat requires a different set of rules. You must keep your craft under control at all times. When approaching a wading angler, you should pass behind that angler as far away and as quietly as possible so as not to disturb the water they are working. If in doubt as to your path, ask the wading angler for their suggestions for an alternate route.

In large lakes, the Delta or in the ocean, ask permission before crowding around a location where other anglers are fishing. There may only be room for one boat or tube at a time in that particular location, so you may have to wait your turn to try your luck.

These "rules" are nothing more than common sense and common courtesy, but it is amazing how many anglers do not stop and think before barging in. Many situations arise for which there may be no specific rule; however, common courtesy and common sense apply in all situations--coupled with treating the water of your fellow angler with the respect it deserves. And, don't forget that the same rules apply to respecting landowners' property! Litterbugs, vandals, fish hogs and poachers ruin fishing privileges for us all.

PHILOSOPHY

Most flyfisherman realize that the whole idea of flyfishing is the deception of live fish--especially trout -- and that by killing their catch, they kill their sport. The sport is the catching, not the killing, and being able to return for yet another day.

Finally, regardless of your fishing success, bring back a limit of litter, for you are the guardians of our streams and of the creatures which inhabit them.

In closing, I reiterate Flycasters' Code of Ethics:

As a member of Flycasters, I will do all in my power to conduct myself in a manner befitting the traditions of our sport of flyfishing.

1. I will follow the Fish and Game laws wherever I fish.

2. I will support conservation practices in order to preserve our natural resources for this and future generations.

3. I will encourage the practice of catch-and-release in all but "put-and-take" waters.

4. I will encourage other fishers, whether they fish with flies or other means, to abide by the same standards as expressed in this Code of Ethics and I pledge to report any violations I observe to the appropriate authorities.

5. I will always remember that my conduct afield is a reflection on our club, its members and our sport; and I will endeavor to conduct myself accordingly.

Let's all try to remember that one of the best things about Flycasters is the fellowship between friends sharing a common experience in a sport we all love.

1. This synopsis was prepared by Bob von Raesfeld and appears in his Beginners' Casting brochure.

About this time, Fenwick was sponsoring a fly-fishing weekend on the Fall River in Northern California where anyone from novices to advanced could be taught to fly-fish or to improve their skills. The teachers were to be Mel Krieger, Gary Borger, Bob Quigley, whose life I once saved on the Fall River, and a couple of others. Since I had a tailing loop problem, I figured they could teach my new girlfriend how to fish and solve my own problem at the same time. On our way up, and remember that this was one of our first weekends away, I had a Lester Flatt and Earl Scruggs playing bluegrass on the tape deck when she announced that she didn't like that music, hit the eject button, took the tape, and threw it up and out of the car through the sunroof. That should have been the first clue. However, someone in my position could overlook many failings.

She learned to fly-fish, and Mel Krieger took one look at my stroke and solved my problem. "Don't punch it," he said. So I was okay, and my new girlfriend took to the sport like a duck to water.

Before and after we got married, she loved to go away on weekends, camp out, and Fly-Fish. She actually became somewhat accomplished. Then the baby came.

She stopped fly-fishing, drinking, and camping. All of a sudden, being outdoors was too dirty and dusty for the baby. So I was back to fly-fishing alone. After a couple of years of this, she announced that she was heading for greener pastures, and I didn't fit into that picture anymore. Divorces were expensive, and after she left on Valentine's Day, I hauled a dumpster up to the house. I got everything she had ever touched and threw it all into the trash. Harsh, but I felt a lot better. The worst part, however, was that she took the fly rods that I had given her over the years.

"But, but," I said, "you quit fly-fishing and haven't used the rods for years. You should leave them."

"Screw you," she said. "I might use them again."

Well, this wonderful woman became my worst nightmare for twenty long years until our daughter graduated from Vassar. Anytime we had a dispute, she always said that we could go back to court to resolve the issue unless we did it her way.

At least I didn't have to go fishing with her again.

The next step in the sequence was when I met my present wife of thirty-three years now. One of the first things I told her was that there were at least three things that I loved to do, and they all started with the letter *F*, and one of those is fishing. I told her that I'd like to take at least one destination trip a year, and if she couldn't deal with all my *F*s and keep me happy, it wouldn't work. Once in a while, she'd go with me.

Although she is not a fisherwoman, she loves to go to the places where trout live because they invariably are found in some of the most beautiful places in the world. This wife is a keeper.

The Next Generation

It is the dream of every serious and contemplative fisherman to pass on the love of the sport and the traditions and customs they have learned over the years to his children who will hopefully someday become the people who will preserve the knowledge of the craft for future generations.

Sometimes, though, as hard as we try, for whatever reason, it doesn't happen.

A good case in point is what happened to a good friend of mine and his daughter. After many years of dunking bait while she was young, she was finally able to handle a fly rod, so my friend planned a trip to the wilds of the Northwest. It was a long drive from California, but a good time was had by the entire family. They found a good motel where he and his wife managed to convince the kids that there really were bears in the closet. I think they all slept with one eye open for the entire stay. They laughed about it today, but then it was a serious business.

My friend wanted to find a place where his daughter could catch a few fish on a fly. It was not an easy task, for most of the water around was serious, so they had to find a place where they could safely wade out a bit and be able to hook a few. The number of fish they took was lost to memory, but that was beside the point. Father and daughter had a wonderful time, and during their stay, they returned several times to their favorite spot. His daughter called it their secret place for many years.

While she was growing up, they fished in many different places together until one day, she told him that she didn't enjoy it anymore and that the only reason she had been doing it was that she thought she could please him. My friend was deeply wounded but didn't say anything because that was her right, and he certainly didn't want to do further damage to what suddenly had turned into a fractured relationship.

After many years of reflection, he had come to realize that not everything in fishing is as he would like it to be. He said that sometimes you don't catch any fish. Sometimes, you catch the big one, and other times, your wishes just don't pan out. As they say in baseball, "You win some, you lose some, and some are rained out." This particular adventure which began with such promise ended in great sadness and was rained out.

The Futaleufú

It's a long way down and a long way back to get to this famous Chilean river with a wonderful name. It starts at the crest of the Andes Mountains and feeds into Lake Yelcho, where the Isla Monita Lodge is located.

ISLA MONITA
Fishing Lodge

Lago Yelcho
PATAGONIA - CHILE

E-Mail: lsmonita@entelchile.net • Alvaro Casanova 287 A - La Reina, Santiago
PHONE: (56-2) 2752198 - (56-2) 6384031 • FAX: (56-2) 2751898 - (56-2) 6381449

Jerry Estruth

Our plane left San Francisco, and after several transfers in Dallas, Santiago, and Puerto Montt, we arrived in Chaitén, where our hosts picked us for the five-hour drive over very muddy roads to our destination, Lake Yelcho and Isla Monita. We were thrilled to no end when our hosts told us that it had rained about 100 inches (no, that's not a misprint) in three days last week. The lake had risen about 30 feet, but the water was beginning to recede and that most of the Futaleufú was fishable. When we got to the small marina where the boats which would take us across to Isla Monita were anchored, we were tired but eager. The lodge was located in the middle of the lake, and to get there, we rode in overloaded wooden boats through rough, windy swells for about thirty minutes. We thought we were dead, but we finally docked and headed up to the lodge. In my experience in South America, no matter how bad the transportation is, rarely does anything bad happen until it does.

The lodge was warm and friendly, and libations were ready and waiting. Tom Parry of New Zealand's fame and I were pleased by the reception we got. Through the windows, we could see a volcano, the rough waters of the lake, and lush flowers growing around the house. Tom and I slept in the same comfortable room where my snoring kept him awake even though he had brought earplugs. At dinner that night, the food was great, and they announced that they had hats and other souvenirs for sale. The hats were $10. That's consistent with my gripe about some lodges. After paying a lot for the trip, they rip you off by charging for a cheap hat.

We were worried about the fishing because the water was so unsettled, but we were assured that it would be okay. The first day, Tom and I went way up the Futaleufú to where it crested the Andes at the Argentinian border.

We put in and fished with a short leader, casting into the bank while we floated. We used a leech and a horsefly with a short dropper behind it. The river was beautiful, and the water had gone down, but the fish were scared, and we didn't take a lot of them on the first day. In fact, the fishing for the entire trip was just mediocre, as it happens sometimes. We couldn't drive to other rivers because they were still blown out, so our fishing was pretty much limited to the Futaleufú and Lake Yelcho and below.

You might think we had a lousy time, but the lodge was so friendly and warm, and the food was so good. We really enjoyed and pampered ourselves. To be in the middle of nowhere and be treated this well was extremely worthwhile.

There was an elegant older couple from the Northeast that made good conversation at mealtimes. They were not good aggressive fisher people anymore, but they showed that they had been in the past. They always dressed to the nines for dinner, unlike the rest of us slobs, and often showed their eccentricities with interesting stories from the past. One day, the woman caught a five-pound brown near the point where the Futaleufú entered Lake Yelcho, and it was the talk of the lodge because no one else had even come close so far.

What I most remember about her was the morning she came out and announced that her husband would be along shortly and that every day, she would wake him by singing:

"Wake up, little birdie,
Wake up, little birdie,
Wake up, little birdie,
All the little birdies are awake
Except the most beautiful birdie of all, so
Wake up, little birdie."

I think we choked on our orange juice, but she was totally sincere and very serious.

By this time, the water level in the lake had dropped about 15 feet, and the fishing improved somewhat, and I nailed a five- to six-pound brown and several more rainbows in the braids before the lake.

The last day we fished the upper river once again and did better than the first time. It was almost a two-hour drive to get to the put in, so the actual float time was limited. We passed through a little town about an hour from the lodge, and I bought a super Chilean wool pull-on hat. Closer to home, we stopped and collected a young lamb that had been slaughtered for our dinner. They dressed it out, flattened it out, and wired it to a rebar frame so it could be roasted. They tilted the frame up against a large rock when we got back to the lodge, built a good fire underneath it, basted it, and let it cook. Yummy, yummy, tickle my tummy. It was great.

This was not the greatest trip I ever took for taking a lot of large fish, but that's the way it goes sometimes. It was memorable for other reasons, not the least of which was the fact that I lost one of my favorite fishing hats in the Santiago Airport. It was embroidered with "Women want Me, Fish fear Me." I would love to find a replacement for that one.

Argentina Again

At the end of January of 2017, Archie Adams, Mac Vought, Larry Kavorous, and I went to Argentina to fish. We flew into Bariloche, which was a beautiful resort area in the middle of the country. January was roughly equivalent to July in the southern hemisphere, so we were there basically in the heat of summertime.

It was kind of a funny trip as we didn't stay in one place for the whole time. We fished with two guides, one of whom had a fine boat and the other one who had a POS (piece of s——). We all fished in both boats, but the one who had the crummy boat couldn't tie knots. I broke off a lot of fish, and after each one, he admonished me for setting the hook too hard. Of course, he ignored the curly end of the leader.

It had rained hard before we got there, and the water was high. So it was high and hot. In short, the fishing was terrible, and between the four of us, I don't think we caught thirty fish in the week we were there. The good news, however, was that the countryside was beautiful. In fact, we had to drive by the Butch Cassidy and the Sundance Kid's residence, where they spent a couple of years after they left the USA and before they met their ends in Bolivia. Interesting stuff.

Butch Cassidy's and Sundance's home

An interesting coincidence was that the Futalefú that we had fished in Chile was also the name of the river we fished in Argentina.

I took a fall in Bariloche as I tripped on a steep and shady staircase on one of the streets. A couple of beautiful university coeds helped me up and asked if I needed help. I thought, *I wish*. I sterilized the wound with the only antiseptic I had, vodka. I put a butterfly on it and refused to get stitches.

It was a long trip to get there and back, and I really decided that I didn't want to make those long international flights to go fishing anymore. This old body won't take it anymore.

Bolivia

Archie called me one day and said that we should go to Bolivia to fish for the elusive payara. He said that it'd be a super trip and that the fishing would be wonderful. He was right on all counts. We all got together in Miami and flew to Laz Paz, Bolivia, before we went on to Santa Cruz. After overnighting there, we boarded a smaller plane for the two-hour flight to our lodge, which was run by Jaime Rodriguez, from Medellin, Colombia, as it turned out. He knew exactly where I had lived for the two years I spent in Medellin.

We flew over the vast Amazonian basin, and it was interesting to look down and see the farms and ranches that dotted the countryside. We arrived at the lodge, and it was very nice.

Since I was a single, I fished with an avid fly fisherman, and it turned out that he was supercompetitive and always glommed on to the front of the boat. That meant that he was able to take the first shot at the holes as we boated along the front of the mangroves. I didn't want to rock the boat, so to speak, as I thought he'd offer to let me have the first spot from time to time.

As it turned out, he didn't do that, and I, as I should have, never brought the subject up.

I caught many fish as it turned out, but the mighty payara only showed up once. It was also called a dogfish because it had very long teeth from its lower jaw.

A large payara and Jerry

The payara was related to the tiger fish in Africa. The fishing was tough. As it turned out, the lodge wasn't fly-fishing only. On alternate weeks, they opened the lodge up for hardware fishermen. The rivers were huge, and it was big water, but the actual water that held fish was pretty well limited. One time, we were wading a bit, and we saw something long and dark in the water. The guide virtually freaked out and got us out of the water. It was a very large electric eel, and the guide said that if it touched us, it could kill us.

The guides had radios, and at one point, Jaime said that some of the others had seen a "tigre" (tiger), which turned out to be a jaguar. What a beautiful animal.

So we caught an amazing number of peacock bass and had a couple of them each day for lunch. They were beautiful and tasty fish.

Tony Botterwick with a nice peacock bass

Many times, we would put on a new fly only to have ravenous and aggressive piranha cut it in half as soon as the fly hit the water.

We also caught a bunch of drumfish called corbina. They had calcium carbonate rocks in their heads, and they rattled them together to attract females for mating. We brought a few of the rocks home for jewelry.

We went back a second time the following year, and at the end of the trip, we decided that we wouldn't go back again because the lodge had continued admitting hardware fishermen.

Although there was a lot of water, the places that could hold payara were few, and hardware guys could really cover the water, and we decided that they were being fished out.

Jaguar tooth for male enhancement

At the lodge, there were several things for sale. I bought a talisman in the form of a necklace that contained a jaguar tooth. The witch doctor who sold it said it could serve as a vehicle for male enhancement.

Jaguar

Piranha

Capybara

So we didn't catch many payara on this trip although we hammered the peacock bass. A couple of interesting things did happen on this trip however. We ate turtle soup prepared by the staff. I asked our guides if they knew what a rubber tree was, and they brought me to one. They called it "gerenge," which was definitely a strange name. They whacked it with a machete, and it immediately started to ooze a white substance, which was certainly latex.

Rubber tree

I got into a lengthy discussion with the staff about their super-stitions, and that was interesting. They talked about "the whistler" who was a being that stalked about at night and killed people. They knew when he was around because he always whistled.

Jaime liked cats. He always had a cat on his lap, and he said that cats did not last too long there as the tigres (jaguars) would catch and eat them. They were no match for the big cats.

Jaime and Moma Cat

Jaime

We'd sit out on the deck of the lodge in the evening, sip rum, and smoke cigars. The most interesting part of this was not the lies told by our friends but looking at the huge jungle and water. Big flocks of birds flew about, and as they would turn as a group, their flocks' profiles were seen, and then as they turned more, their profiles would disappear.

The lodge was situated a long way from the water's edge, and the high-water mark was at least 50 feet higher and came up almost to the lodge.

Jaime told us that there have always been people in the Amazon basin, meaning for thousands of years. He said that when they were building the lodge, which was beautiful, they dug up many pots.

Ancient pottery

Duncan Brothers, Alaska
The Chosen River, AKA
The Kanectok

The frozen north was always beckoning. Archie, Mac, Doug, Larry, and Stanley, all good fishing buddies from Russia, were talking to me about a fabulous fishing lodge called the Duncan Brothers on the Chosen River in Alaska. To get there, I would have to fly to Anchorage, spend the night there, get on another plane, and fly to Bethel, where you would spend another night. Then you needed to get on another plane and fly thirty minutes south to get to Quinhagak. There the Duncans would pick you up, put you on jet boats, and motor up the river for about two hours to finally get to the lodge.

After listening for several years about how great this place was, I decided to go and see what it's all about. I flew to Anchorage, where I met up with an old Peace Corps buddy named Lou Jarussi. He was famous back in the day because he was stopped at a light in Bogota next to an open-slatted cattle truck. It was an unusually warm day, and Lou had the window of his jeep down, and one of the cows took a projection dump out of the truck into and through Lou's open window.

He and I had a nice dinner, and I was off to the Bethel metropolis the next morning. Actually, there was not much of a reason to go there.

The next morning, even though we wouldn't be fishing for a while, we all put on our waders because the trip on the jet boat would be cold.

The put in on the Chosen River

Going upriver, we saw bald eagles, beavers, moose, and other assorted animals. It was a beautiful day, but I was having trouble breathing. When we got to the camp, we found our hard-sided tents and got organized. I was bunking with Archie, and he mentioned that he had "stuff," and I had "shit." He was quoting George Carlin, and we had a good laugh about that. I was still breathing hard, and we were worried about that.

We were ten men, and some of them went fishing that afternoon. I rested and rigged up my poles. That night, we met our guides and had an orientation talk from Clint Duncan. The Duncans had been running this camp for a very long time, and it was beautiful. He warned us about bears and talked about treating the fish well. I felt right at home.

To summarize the camp, we had great food, good guides, fine boats, and superb fishing. This 2020 will be my sixth trip there, and I'm looking forward to it. In August, the kings, chub, humpies, silvers, and reds are all in the river spawning and dying. The 2020 trip was cancelled due to the Wuhan Flu.

We weren't interested in the salmon, except for the silvers that were still fresh and hit hard and fought well. What we were looking for were the Dolly Vardens, the rainbows, and the grayling.

In the mornings, we would fish with beads and attack the Dollies. It was not uncommon to catch and release over a hundred of them in the morning. A lot of times, we'd pick up rainbows to 25 inches because they were feeding along with the Dollies. Many times, we'd pick up some graylings. Graylings were beautiful fish, and they grew very slowly. An eighteen-inch fish could be up to twenty years old. A lot of us veterans of the Russian and Mongolian verminators started using mice patterns. The rainbows and even the graylings loved them. We got so excited that we started "mouse offs" for some competition. Mac Vought, a super serious mouser now only fishes with mice flies.

Grayling

Because the Native Americans really owned the river, the Duncans made an accommodation to preserve the pristine quality of the river. The jet boats would only run between eight and nine in the mornings and between five and six in the afternoons. If any boat was not back at camp by six, they'd send out other boats to look for you on the assumptions that you were in some kind of trouble. In all the years I've been going, our motor only failed once.

Except for the years that Jeff Wilkes of frigate bird fame came with us, I have fished with Archie or Rufous, good fishermen all!

Rufous and a silver salmon

Jerry's beautiful leopard rainbow

Jerry and Archie with a silver salmon double

A couple of special things always happened in the cook tent.

Breakfast was served at 7:00 a.m., but coffee was on at 5:30 a.m. Those of us who are early risers could gather about 6:00 a.m. and tell lies and jokes. Larry Kavorus, who was a fighter pilot in Nam, had a great memory for jokes and kept us all laughing. Every one of our group was a good fisherman and well traveled. Since most of us had fished together for years, it was a fun time.

When we would get off the river, we'd usually have an hour or so before dinner. We'd sit around, smoke cigars, eat wonderful salmon hors d'oeuvres, and sample ample adult beverages.

Our quarters

We had hot showers and heated tents, so we were always comfortable.

One year, Archie and I went to a large flat pool and skated dry flies for large Dollies. We made ourselves tired because we caught so many fish over 25 inches.

Health is always a worry when we are so far removed from medical facilities. I mentioned that I was getting out of breath. That problem only got worse as the week progressed. When I got back to Tucson, I was not in good shape. It turned out that my oxygen level was 82 percent, and I had a very large pulmonary embolism for the second time and was sent immediately to a hospital. It turned out that I needed a pacemaker and some Xarelto, a mega blood thinner.

Last year on the next to the last day, Archie was returning from fishing a braid and suddenly had chest pains. Fortunately, he had some nitroglycerine pills with him, and he got better; however, he left the camp a day early and finally got back to Wichita, where he got a couple of stents and a pacemaker.

As I get older and it becomes harder to wade a stream, the comfort of having good boats and good guides becomes more important. I think I'll fish at the Duncans until I can't anymore.

Poems and Prayers

"The charm of fishing is that it is the pursuit of what's elusive but attainable and a perpetual series of occasions for hope."

Here's a poem found hanging on the wall of Mill Cottage on the River Test:

Late in the second week of May
When mayfly take their holiday,
Tired of pursuing lesser fry,
I sallied forth resolved to try
For one of these great super trout
That Alf had recently put out.
Soon I found one, there he lay
Under a tussock in a bay
Like a great lining in the stream,
Nine inches draught, six in his beam
Watching in wonderment and awe,
The largest trout I ever saw.
I spoke aloud a foolish wish,
"I'd sell my soul to catch that fish."
I'd hardly spoken when I spied
A total stranger at my side.
Who said, "If that's the way you feel,
I'm quite prepared to do a deal.
My name, Sir, is Beelzebub,
Tho not a member of your club,
Amongst you, I have lately found
A promising recruiting ground.

The younger folk I tempt to Hades
With cocktails, cards, and pretty ladies.
But when it comes to older members
Whose vital fires have sunk to embers
Failing inducement of the flesh
Whereby the older members can
(Provided they're prepared to sign
This form upon the dotted line)
Catch anything they care to fish for.
What more can these old busters wish for?
I think you'll find it worth your while
To give my scheme a little trial."
Now from the corner of my eye,
I'd seen some mayflies floating by
So shouting, "Damn, Sir, your help's not needed."
I hooked him but was promptly weeded.
I slackened line, I pulled it tight,
From right to left, from left to right.
T'was shortly clear, I might as well
Have hooked the Grosvenor Hotel.
Beelzebub, who all the while,
Had watched with an indulgent smile
Said, "So he's weeded you, the bounder!
He looked about a seven pounder.
Perhaps in view of his resistance,
May now I offer my assistance?"
And with a merry little caper,
He proffered me a pen and paper.
Seized with desire to conscience blind,
I took the fountain pen and signed.
When prompted by some devilish urge,
I saw the leviathan emerge
And said serenely alongside
Like Queen Mary on the tide,
And there I must admit the Nick
Was both resourceful, cute, and quick

For stooping low about the whale.
He gaffed the monster with his tail,
Remarking as he wiped the sting.
"This is a handy little thing,
And now, Sir, let me shake your hand
As one of our devoted band
We'll give you in a year or so
A nice warm welcome down below.
Meanwhile, it's been a fruitful stroll.
You've caught your fish, and I've caught a soul.
Ha-ha, excuse me my little joke!"
He gave my ribs a playful poke, and in a panic, I awoke.

Haven't We All Been Tempted?

(Found in Dick Frazier's lodge New Zealand, 1986)

I pray that I may live to fly-fish
Until my dying day
And when it comes to my last cast
I then most humbly pray
When in the Lord's great landing net
And peacefully asleep
That, in his mercy, I be judged
Good enough to keep.

(I recited this at Dave Oke's memorial service.)

Afterword

Okay, now you've heard the stories, it's time to write your own.

If you're young, you should plan your fishing trips well.

If you're older, you should write them down and talk about your trips with youngsters.

You can do worse than have a lifetime love affair chasing fish.

Natasha

Mac in Russia

Dick Frazier's lodge

Signposts

Beautiful leopard rainbows

"Larry's" last fish

A happy Archie

About the Author

The author has been fly-fishing for over seventy years. The book contains stories about some of the adventures that have happened over that time. He has been fishing all over the world from South America, New Zealand, Russia, and Mongolia. You'll have fun with the stories and the sights he has seen. You'll hear about him and his friends, many of whom have sadly passed on.

The author loves the sport and has met many fine people along the way.

CPSIA information can be obtained
at www.ICGtesting.com
Printed in the USA
LVHW020931110221
678898LV00010B/913